"Once you learn to read,
    you will be forever free."

Frederick Douglass

Author's Note

This book is a fictional account of several episodes from Frederick Douglass's childhood. The story imagines what might have happened, based on *The Narrative of the Life of Frederick Douglass* and historical facts about both Douglass and the time period in which he lived.

Turning the Page: Frederick Douglass Learns to Read
Editors: Jane Hileman and Gina Cline
Author: Amanda Hamilton Roos
Illustrator: Michael Adams
Book Designer: Kristina Rupp
Production Director: Robbie Byerly
Project Director: Jayson Fleischer

First Edition, January 2014
ISBN: 978-1-61406-683-5, 1-61406-683-3
eISBN: 978-1-61406-710-8, 1-61406-710-4
10 9 8 7 6 5 4

Copyright © 2014 by American Reading Company®

Turning the Page

Frederick Douglass Learns to Read

Written by Amanda Hamilton Roos
Illustrated by Michael Adams

Turning the Page

Frederick Douglass Learns to Read

Frederick Douglass was born into slavery sometime in the early 1800s. Frederick lived on a large plantation in Maryland that used the labor of enslaved African American people to grow tobacco and other crops. People were bought and sold like property and forced to work from sunup to sundown, with no pay. Parents and children, husbands and wives were often separated, never to see each other again.

Like many other enslaved children, Frederick didn't know his father, his birthday, or even how old he was. Although Frederick and his mother, Harriet, were separated when he was just a baby, he always remembered the way she would hold him and call him her little valentine. Harriet was also one of the few enslaved Black women who knew how to read.

When he was about seven or eight years old, Frederick's life changed. A couple in Baltimore City named Mr. and Mrs. Auld asked to borrow Frederick from his master. They wanted him to take care of their young son, Thomas.

Baltimore was a port city with ships and people arriving every day from all over the world. Most of the African American people living in Baltimore at this time were free. There were Black churches, Black businesses, and Black schools. Life for enslaved Black people was often better in the city, as well. With so many neighbors watching, many were better clothed, better fed, and better treated. While Frederick was sent to Baltimore as a slave, the city would become the first stop on his journey to freedom.

One windy afternoon, Frederick arrived in Baltimore Harbor on a ship packed with sheep. As he climbed onto the wharf, he could already tell that life here would be different. People of every shade hurried by, well dressed and full of purpose. Carriages, wagons, carts all clattered by, packed with goods. With the salty scent of the sea, even the air smelled different. Different might mean better, Frederick thought. He couldn't imagine a life worse than the one he'd left behind.

He set off into the city, following one of the sailors to the Aulds' home.

Arriving at the Aulds' door, Frederick saw the whole family waiting to meet him: Mr. Auld, Mrs. Auld, and small Thomas, peeking from behind his mother's skirts.

"Hello, dear," said Mrs. Auld, with a gentle smile. Frederick could barely reply. Never had a White person spoken to him with such warmth. Could this be his new mistress?

It was. Frederick soon learned that Mrs. Auld had been born and raised in the North, where slavery was outlawed. To her, Frederick was a person, not property, and she treated him as she would want to be treated. She smiled at him, spoke kindly to him, even invited him to watch her sing.

Frederick was unsure how to react to this kindness. Though grateful to be away from the brutality of the plantation, he knew that nothing had really changed. He watched as little Thomas ran about, gleefully ignoring his mother's instructions. Frederick knew he would never be allowed to disobey Mrs. Auld. Life at the Aulds' might be more comfortable, but Frederick wanted more from life than kindness and clean clothes. Unless he did something, he would be a slave for life. But what could he, as a child, do?

One day, Mrs. Auld handed Frederick an open book. "Frederick, do you know how to read?"

"No, Ma'am." Frederick shook his head. He didn't want to tell her that children on the plantation didn't learn to read.

"Well, let's start with the A, B, Cs."

Frederick was an eager learner. He loved to trace the crisp, black letters with his finger, committing each one to memory. He raced through the alphabet. Mrs. Auld rejoiced in his success.

One day, Mr. Auld discovered them reading together.

"What are you doing?!" demanded Mr. Auld. "Are you teaching Frederick to read? You must stop at once."

"But, Husband..." Mrs. Auld looked shocked.

"My dear, you must understand," Mr. Auld explained. "It is against the law to teach a slave to read. And for good reason. It will do him no good. Learning will spoil him. He will become unhappy with his place. You will make him unfit to be a slave. He will start to want freedom."

Mrs. Auld wouldn't meet Frederick's eyes. Reluctantly, she gathered up the books and put them away.

As for Frederick, Mr. Auld's words sank deep into his heart.

That night, Frederick couldn't sleep.
Mr. Auld's words kept replaying in his head.
As long as he could remember, Frederick had
struggled to understand how it was that one group
of people could enslave others. He considered Mr.
Auld's words. Was Mr. Auld telling the truth? Why
would reading spoil him? And why did Mr. Auld say
that reading would make a slave unhappy in his place?
Frederick was already unhappy.

Outside the window, Frederick saw the moon peek out
from behind the clouds. A shaft of brilliant light struck
the distant water of the harbor.

Mr. Auld wanted to keep Frederick enslaved. Frederick
was determined to free himself. Mr. Auld had clearly
said that a person who could read would be unfit to be a
slave. Frederick knew he wasn't meant to be a slave. This
was it! The pathway from slavery to freedom was clear.
No matter what, he would learn to read.

Mrs. Auld had decided something, too. The next morning, instead of offering to read to him after breakfast, she said, "Boy, run out and get the firewood. Don't be lazy!" It was the first time Mrs. Auld had talked to him with such coldness, and he felt something inside him being twisted and squeezed.

The days became weeks, and Mrs. Auld became more and more intent on undoing what she had done. Whenever he moved slowly, she yelled at him. Whenever he touched a book, she snatched it away.

It was too late. In introducing Frederick to reading, Mrs. Auld had lit a spark she could never put out. Each time she yelled at him, she only fanned the flames. He might have lost his teacher, but he was determined to find a way to learn to read.

A few weeks later, Mrs. Auld sent Frederick to the grocery store. He was often sent on errands for the Aulds, errands that took him all over Baltimore. He saw people young and old, Black and White, with books, newspapers, pamphlets. Everywhere he went, people could read. But not Frederick.

Frederick scowled as he walked. He was determined to keep his promise to himself. He kicked the ground and watched the pebbles scatter before him. How would he learn without a teacher?

Today, his route took him down a back alley behind the grocery store. Frederick watched a White boy about his age playing alone. The boy's schoolbook lay discarded on the cobblestones beside him. Frederick noticed the boy's faded clothes. He got an idea.

"Hi," Frederick said nervously. "What are you doing?"

"Nothing really. My mama says I'm not to come home until dinner. She says to stay out of the way and just wait for dinner."

Frederick remembered the bread he had in his pocket. He knew that the poor White children in his neighborhood were often hungry. Living with the wealthy Aulds, Frederick had plenty of food.

"Look here, I have some bread," Frederick said, pulling a roll from his pocket. "You can have it if you'll show me your book."

"What? This book here?" The boy picked up the forgotten book. "You don't want to see that. It's only my school primer."

"Just the same," Frederick repeated, "I'd trade you some bread for it."

"Ha! You got a deal!" the boy said eagerly, handing it over. "But," he added, "you got to return it. If I don't bring it to school tomorrow, I'll get beat."

Frederick opened the book with trembling hands.

"You know how to read?" asked the little boy, through a mouth full of bread.

"No, I don't."

"What? You don't know any words?"

"Not that one," Frederick said, pointing to the first page.

"Oh, well, that one is easy. Here, let me show you."

And with that, Frederick had his first new teacher.

Later, as Frederick returned to the Aulds' home, he was filled with hope about his new plan. He knew Mrs. Auld would be waiting, ready to lash out at him. But beyond the Aulds, beyond Baltimore, he could see the vast, open sea, wild and full of promise.

Afterword

For Frederick, this was just the beginning.
He turned many of the young White boys in Baltimore
into his teachers and learned to read and write.

When he was about 20 years old, after multiple attempts,
Frederick finally escaped slavery for good.

As an adult, Frederick worked tirelessly for the abolition
of slavery and was a champion for the rights of both
African Americans and women of all races. Not only did
Frederick learn to read, he spent the rest of his life using
words to fight for the freedom of all people. He was
one of America's greatest speakers, writers, and thinkers,
changing the world with his voice and pen.

A special thanks to Dr. Ka'mal McClarin
for lending his expertise to this project.

Dr. McClarin is the curator of the
Frederick Douglass National Historic Site in Washington, D.C.

Visit the Frederick Douglass National Historical Site to explore Douglass's
home, Cedar Hill, and to learn more about this amazing American.

http://www.nps.gov/frdo/index.htm

About the Text

This story is a work of historical fiction. As such, although much of the information is true, some specific events described here are inventions of the author. All information about Baltimore City, Maryland, and the conditions of slavery are accurate. The information about Frederick Douglass's early life, his move to Baltimore, and the methods by which he learned to read are based on the facts he himself reported about his life. In his narrative, Douglass does not describe his initial inspiration for the plan to use White boys as his reading teachers, nor does he describe any "first" encounter. This story imagines one way this might have happened.

About the Illustrations

Michael Adams did extensive research to create the illustrations in this book. In addition to interpreting this text, he also read the early chapters of *The Narrative of the Life of Frederick Douglass, an American Slave*, written by Douglass 20 years after this story takes place. Professor Adams looked into a variety of subject matter related to the era, including the troubling reality of slavery in the 1820s; agriculture in Talbot County, Maryland; and the port city of Baltimore. The landscape, architecture, and clothing are based on references from museums, historical societies, and paintings from that period. Adams included some very specific subject matter, like the Baltimore oriole, the state flower (black-eyed Susan), and the *Pride of Baltimore* schooner.

Checklist for Success

A Pilot's Guide to the Successful Airline Interview

by Cheryl A. Cage

Layout/Editing by Pam Ryan

Cover Design by Alexander Cannon

Checklist for Success:
A Pilot's Guide to the Successful Airline Interview
Cheryl A. Cage

Cover Design by Alexander Cannon
Layout and editing by Pam Ryan
Seventh Printing 2001, Eighth Printing (Revised) 2002
Sixth Printing - Fourth Revision - 2000
Fourth Printing 1997 - 3rd Revision, Fifth Printing 1999
Third Printing 1996 - 2nd Revision
Second Printing 1995
First Printing 1994
Copyright 1994, 1996, 1997, 1999, 2000, 2001, 2002 - Cheryl Cage

Printed in the United States of America
Published by Cage Consulting

Library of Congress Catalog Card Number: 94-92311
ISBN 0-9642839-0-5

Disclaimer: This book is sold with the understanding that the publisher and the author are not engaged in rendering legal or medical services. If legal or medical expert assistance is required, the services of a competent professional should be sought.

This book is a general information book on preparing for an airline pilot interview. It is understood that the information contained in this book does not guarantee success. The author and publisher shall have neither liability nor responsibility to any person or entity with respect to any loss or damage caused, or alleged to be caused directly or indirectly by the information contained in this book.

If you do not wish to be bound by the above, you may return this book to the publisher for a full refund.

Table of Contents

Visit our website!
http://www.cageconsulting.com

CALL US TOLL FREE: **1-888-899-CAGE**

Contact Cage Consulting

Thinking about taking advantage of
Cage Consulting's Pilot Interview Preparation Services?

- *Full Interview Preparation Services for all carriers (in person or by telephone)*
- *Special Concerns Consulting*
- *Career Consulting*
- *Technical Classes*

To learn more about our services or to set an appointment please call
1-888-899-CAGE
(toll free)

Interested in Other Cage Consulting Pilot Study Guides?

- *Airline Pilot Technical Interviews: A Study Guide (McElroy)*
- *Mental Math for Pilots (McElroy)*
- *Reporting Clear? (Cage)*
- *Checklist Interactive CD: An Interview Simulator (Cage)*
- *Pilot E-Training Test: Mental Math (Cage/McElroy)*
- *Problem Solved: Ten Steps to Better Management of Mistakes, Problems, and Conflicts (Cage)*

To view each title, or to order online, please visit our website at
www.cageconsulting.com
You may also call our toll free number, 1-888-899-CAGE, to order!

Check our website often for new products and special articles!
www.cageconsulting.com

FOREWORD

by W. H. Traub
Vice President
Flight Standards and Training (Ret.)
United Airlines

I have had the honor of participating in the hiring program for a major airline for almost twenty years. During that period of time I have found that, for a pilot applicant, the most difficult step of the selection process is the interview phase. You might wonder why an applicant with superb technical skills and excellent experience is turned down due to an inability to interview successfully. In *Checklist for Success* you will learn why airlines consider the interview phase of the selection process to be such an important step in the overall evaluation of applicants. Let me quote a very compelling paragraph found in this book:

> ". . . solid technical skills do not always guarantee the best overall candidate. For example, in one National Aeronautics and Space Administration (NASA) investigation, over 60 accidents where crew-coordination played a significant role were studied. . . . Common factors among these accidents included: preoccupation with minor technical problems, inadequate leadership, failure to delegate tasks and assign responsibilities, failure to set priorities, inadequate monitoring, failure to utilize available data, and failure to communicate intent and plans. The National Transportation Safety Board (NTSB) estimates that these 'human factors' contribute to 70% to 80% of airplane crashes."

Over the years I've had the opportunity to talk to a number of candidates about the employment process, some after an unsuccessful interview. All of the advice that I could provide is contained in this book in a very well written format. Your careful reading and study of this material, although it cannot guarantee success, will certainly enhance your chances.

Let me provide one other very important quote from the book:

> "An employee with a positive attitude is invaluable to any employer. . . . A positive attitude lays the groundwork for good communication and positive team interaction."

Again, this is very sound advice and is exactly what we are looking for in the hiring process.

By considering *Checklist for Success* you have taken an important step toward improving your competitiveness, which will increase your chances of being hired into one of the most rewarding, best professions available.

W. H. Traub

INTRODUCTION TO
THE 2002 EDITION OF *CHECKLIST*

Airline pilot interviewers are constantly critiquing the interviewing process. They ask themselves: are the interview questions reaping insight or are some approaches that have worked well for years suddenly passé? What new traits have been discovered to be important to the pilot position? Is the interviewing process enough of a "surprise" to the applicant as to spur real discussion and not just canned answers?

With the incredible "gouge" available to any pilot applicant, interviewers constantly subtract questions that are becoming too well known, in addition to developing new areas of discussion that will enhance the process.

Having said this: don't panic! The interviewing process has not gone through extreme re-write!

The interviewing process requires the *same approach* I have been counseling since 1988: *self-evaluation*. In order to clearly define yourself for an interviewer you must take the time to critique every area of your personal and professional life. Only through these exercises of self-critique will you be able to discuss (with someone you have never met – the pilot interviewer) your personal approach in any area.

What you will find in this new edition of *Checklist* is an even clearer overall picture of how you need to prepare for your interviews. Throughout the book I offer new approaches our clients have found particularly helpful in clarifying the process.

It has been extremely gratifying for me to know that Cage Consulting's books have become, for many, required tools for use in preparing for the competitive world of pilot interviewing. As a participant in one of the most competitive industries in the world you know the delicious agony of pursuing, and ultimately achieving, a difficult goal. As a publisher and writer one of my goals has been to complete a work that would positively impact the lives of others. And, due to the success of our books and services (primarily through word-of-mouth) I am going to allow myself to think, just maybe, I have reached a small part of my goal in this particular corner of the world.

As always, I love hearing from you. Only through my reader's honest critique will I be able to increase the quality of our books and services.

Cheryl A. Cage
Tuscon, Arizona
2002

INTRODUCTION TO THE FIRST EDITION

The decision to write this workbook came from a simple, but difficult situation. In 1988, I developed an Airline Pilot Interview Preparation Program. Happily, this program seemed to bring success to more than a few of my clients. Through referrals from this first group of pilot clients my phone started ringing. A client list, which was small and manageable in 1989 became overwhelming in 1990. Since I worked with each and every client I found myself having to say, "My calendar is full and I am unable to take any new clients at this time." It was either that or work 7 days a week, 18 hours a day. (I tried that for a few months, and I do not recommend it!)

Every time I had to say no I felt terrible. I found myself in this uncomfortable situation more often than I care to remember and finally came to the conclusion that although I couldn't clone myself, I could clone my program. I decided to put the program in workbook form. My objective was to design a manual which would allow pilots to prepare for airline interviews on their own. I wanted to write a "user friendly" manual that could be referred to by pilots of *any experience level*. This workbook is the result.

THE PROCESS Cage Consulting began as a general job search service. My clients were professionals from all fields. My introduction to working with pilots came when I offered my resume services to a small group of pilots living in the Denver area. These pilots had recently lost their jobs due to the bankruptcy of their airline.

While working with these individuals I sensed a pervasive belief that technical background and experience were all that was needed to secure a new airline job. This was outdated thinking and it disturbed me.

That distress proved legitimate. Even with the wealth of experience these professional pilots had to offer, without exception this group was unsuccessful in their initial attempts at landing new cockpit positions.

What these pilots had failed to understand was that the selection process had changed over the years. Flight departments were no longer just searching for people with technical proficiency in flying. Airlines were interested in hiring individuals with highly developed management, communication, and team-player skills *in addition to* technical skills.

Flight departments are no longer just searching for people with technical proficiency in flying.

To discuss one's abilities in these introspective areas required a different kind of preparation than these pilots had ever experienced.

Having watched these professionals stumble—and not wanting to see it happen to others—I was motivated to develop my Pilot Interview Preparation Program, and ultimately to write *Checklist For Success: A Pilot's Guide to the Successful Airline Interview.*

The initial program in 1988 was based on my work with business professionals, discussions with pilot interviewers at the major airlines, and my own airline background. Since 1989 the program has been continually reviewed, updated, and expanded. I have discussed the interviewing process with flight officer interviewers, chief pilots, and aviation medical experts. I have spent many, many hours debriefing my clients after their interviews.

This workbook will take you from application and resume preparation through to the actual interview. It is my sincere hope that the information included in this workbook will make your journey to the cockpit a bit easier.

Cheryl Cage
Aurora, Colorado 1994

PLEASE READ!

In preparing for an interview you will discover a great deal of "simple" advice (for example: provide all applicable documentation when discussing a problem area; keep your resume to one page; wear a suit; never say "I have no answer to that question"). Each piece of "simple" advice is like a piece of a jigsaw puzzle. Taken separately they can be confusing. Put them all together and the picture becomes clear.

Although I have worked hard to present this advice and information in a logical order, there are times when a comment may seem out of place in Chapter 1, only to make perfect sense upon completing Chapter 3.

For this reason I ask that you read the entire workbook before beginning your chapter-by-chapter preparation.

AIRLINE INTERVIEWS This workbook is written from the perspective of interviewing with a major carrier. However, the same approach should be used for any pilot interview.

HE or SHE? For no other reason than clarity, masculine pronouns are used throughout this workbook.

UPDATES *Checklist* is updated every 12-18 months.

Chapter 1

GETTING THE INTERVIEW

Waiting for an interview with a major airline can be a frustrating and anxiety-ridden experience. During this waiting period, trips to the mailbox take on a whole new dimension.

Applicants invited to an interview are selected based on criteria deemed important by the individual airline. This "to interview" criteria basically consists of concrete information such as flight time, type of flight jobs held, ratings, and education. This criteria can change depending on the experience level of the available applicants. It is important to remember that your application is constantly being judged BASED ON THE COMPETITION AT THE TIME.

Your application is constantly being judged BASED ON THE COMPETITION AT THE TIME.

A clear example of this fact: in 1982 Braniff became the first major airline to go into bankruptcy. Until that time, the majority of major airline pilot applicants came from the military, commuter airlines, and corporate flight departments. Because of the seniority system, it was virtually unheard of to have an airline pilot leave one carrier to start over with another. Deregulation, the tidal wave of bankruptcies, and the airlines' newly enlightened view of "seasoned" pilots changed all that.

After 1982, the traditional applicant (who came directly from the military or the commuter/corporate world) became overshadowed by the scores of experienced ex-airline pilots flooding the market. It was not unusual for these ex-airline pilots to have 20 years of airline experience and over 10,000 hours of flying time. Because the airlines had this abundance of highly qualified applicants to choose from, not surprisingly, the traditional pilot-applicants were put on the bottom of the "to interview" list. The high experience level of these displaced airline pilots caused the CRITERIA for being invited for an interview to change.

The hiring situation of the last decade has been a new experience for the airline industry. However, the same basic premise is a constant within the "to interview" selection process. If you are a pilot with a bachelors degree, 1500 hours of flight time, and in your first year of working for a commuter, but the majority of available pilot applicants possess a bachelors degree, 2,500 hours, and three years of commuter experience you can assume that you will not be selected for an interview UNTIL THOSE APPLICANTS HAVE BEEN REVIEWED.

INCREASING YOUR ODDS

For these reasons it is imperative that you continue to update your skills and background. You must never stop working to increase your marketability. Some ideas:

- Keep flying and building your hours

- Earn additional ratings and certifications

- If you are in the military, earn your civilian ratings

- Continue to upgrade at the earliest possible time

- Complete your bachelors degree or higher education degrees

In addition to specific training and education there are other steps you can take that may help put your name closer to the top of an airline's "to interview" list.

- Find out if there are any "airline specific" steps you can take to increase your chances for an interview (for example: a letter of recommendation from a pilot or other employee).

Make sure you ask the right people if a particular process is acceptable. One of my clients was given the advice from a company pilot to "just take your application to the employment office and wait until someone will talk to you." Luckily, my client asked around and discovered that this type of action was actually looked upon as overly aggressive and not very polite. Someone within the Personnel Department would have been the logical person to ask if this approach was acceptable.

- If a company pilot offers to hand-carry your application into the employment office, make sure you know how this individual is viewed by the company!

I had one client who had his application hand-carried to the airline's employment office by a senior captain. Unfortunately, he found out too late that this captain had been involved in numerous altercations with the employment office concerning applicants he felt should be hired. (Although this client was not harmed in this particular instance, it caused him a great deal of concern and many sleepless nights.)

There is no magic formula for securing an interview.

- Update your applications on a regular basis. Be sure to follow the airline's update schedule. If they allow an update once every six months, do not send a new application every three months!
- By all means exploit your network! If the brother of your college roommate's wife is the V.P. of Flight Operations for an airline you want to work for—seek an introduction!

There is no magic formula for securing an interview. However, by following these steps you can rest at night knowing you are doing everything possible to get your foot in the door.

Notes

Chapter 2

9 STEPS TO A SUCCESSFUL INTERVIEW

Prior to and during an interview there are all kinds of unknowns facing an applicant. What EXACT questions will be asked? Will the interviewer be friendly or aggressive? What am I going to do if a question is asked and I don't know the answer? Add to these concerns the intense competition and the fact that, no matter how structured the process appears, the human element is always involved and there is no doubt—interviewing is stressful.

Interview preparation must be approached in a logical manner.

Every applicant wants to know what to expect when they sit down in an interview chair. Every applicant wants to understand how to avoid the most common mistakes. Every applicant wants to feel comfortable discussing weaknesses while at the same time stressing individual strengths. Every applicant wants to walk out of the interview saying, "Well, I did my very best."

These *are* attainable goals! But, as with flight training, the learning process must be approached in a logical manner.

This logical process consists of nine basic steps. To be fully prepared for a pilot interview you must:

1. Understand the reasoning behind the pilot interviewing process.

2. Become familiar with the roles of the people involved in the process.

3. Gain an awareness of the most common interviewing mistakes.

4. Determine what life experiences (both positive and negative) best describe your individual personality.

5. Learn how to discuss your life experiences in a complete, yet concise manner.

6. Practice your verbal delivery.

---

7. Study for the technical side of the interview.

8. Prepare your physical appearance to ensure a professional impression.

9. Make sure all your paperwork is complete and accurate.

Notice that nowhere have I listed "memorize the answers to the questions." (This statement, obviously, does not apply to technical questions which require memorization of certain facts, figures, and approaches to problem solving.)

There is a great deal of airline interviewing advice that suggests the best way to prepare for a pilot interview is to collect a list of all possible interview questions and memorize the answers that have received the most positive responses from interviewers. I suppose that might work if you were the first person to present these answers, but you won't be.

Memorization of answers is NOT the way to prepare for your interview.

It is important to remember that although there are thousands of pilot applicants, there are a limited number of major carrier interviewers. This limited number of interviewers talk to the thousands of pilot applicants. And, never forget that interviewers talk among themselves. It is only a matter of hearing the same answer to a specific question two or three times before the interviewers tag the answer as rote. It becomes obvious that the applicant is parroting an answer that someone else told them would work. No matter how good the answer is, the applicant is given negative marks for using it. This "parroting" can sneak its way into your thinking even if you have made a sincere effort not to prepare in this manner.

It is important to debrief those pilots who have been through a specific airline interview process. It is helpful to discover the format of the interview and to learn the types of questions, both technical and personal, that are asked. You can learn a great deal just by listening to an applicant's overall impression of a specific airline's interview process.

However, you must be aware that problems can arise when your friend goes beyond sharing his overall impressions and begins recounting the answers that he gave to specific questions.

Human nature being what it is, the majority of the answers he will share with you will sound terrific—remember, he's had time to embellish and revise his answers (we all employ a little revisionist history when asked about a job interview).

Another problem encountered by the memorized type of preparation is that it is impossible to list every question that could be asked! Even if you learn answers for 200 questions, Murphy's Law is that you will probably be asked question #201!

I had a young client who was firm in his desire to prepare question-by-question. No matter how hard I tried I could not get him to look at the big picture. After his interview he called me. The first thing he said to me was, "I understand now what you were trying to get me to do." During his interview he waited, with wonderful answer in hand, for the question, "What do you believe are the five components of a positive leadership style?" Instead he was asked, "How do you lead?" Because he had thought of leadership only in the form of a list that would answer a specific question, he had a great deal of trouble making the shift to talking in broad terms about his basic leadership outlook. He became flustered and, unfortunately, from that point on felt very uncomfortable and could never seem to get back on track. He was not offered a position.

You can stop sounding like everyone else by thinking in broad terms about your individual outlook and experiences. By reviewing and dissecting those personal experiences which taught you specific lessons (about leadership, communication, handling conflicts, etc.) you will be prepared to discuss any area an interviewer may wish to review. By giving only examples of situations that have happened to you, no one will be able to accuse you of being anything other than yourself.

You can stop sounding like everyone else by thinking in broad terms about your individual outlook and experiences.

Notes

Chapter 3

DEMYSTIFYING THE PROCESS

"Why are they interested in THAT?"

This is a common question from a new client. Almost without exception during the introduction to "Self-Evaluation" (Chapter 6) and "Information Gathering" (Chapter 9), etc., new clients look at me and sigh, "Why is this so hard"?

"Why are they interested in THAT?" is an understandable question. And an important one to answer.

The pilot who has been invited to an interview has spent years pursuing flight time, ratings, and certifications. Innumerable hours and countless dollars have been sacrificed to acquire the technical knowledge needed to fly an aircraft. Because of this technical emphasis it is unnerving for many applicants to discover the interview tends to focus on areas that appear to be, at first, not related to aviation at all. Yes, there are technical questions and simulator rides, but the majority of questions encompass personality traits and individual outlook. Questions are asked that allow critical analysis of how an individual pilot will approach various real-world interpersonal situations.

"Why are they asking me about interpersonal situations?"

The emphasis placed on the "non-technical" side of the interview does NOT mean that a poor technical pilot with strong interpersonal skills will look more desirable to an employer. Obviously the technical skills must be present to proceed through the process.

The interviewer asks these types of questions because he needs to become comfortable with an applicant's personal approach and outlook. The interview process is designed to allow the interviewer to become knowledgeable about both the applicant's technical expertise and the applicant's communication style, leadership abilities, decision making processes, problem solving approach and team orientation skills. It is important that the interviewer gain a strong comfort level with an applicant's overall attitude towards their profession and life in general.

Many of my clients have come from the "displaced pilot" category. I have listened to these pilots talk about how they were hired the first time, often 20 or even 30 years before. "I just sat down with the chief pilot and we talked airplanes" is a common theme. "They reviewed my background and experience, I flew the simulator, was asked a few questions, and pretty soon we were talking class dates."

Research in flight crew training and the advances in technology over the past two decades have shown the aviation community that solid technical skills do not always guarantee the best overall candidate. For example, in one National Aeronautics and Space Administration (NASA) investigation (1968–1976), over 60 accidents where crew-coordination played a significant role were studied. Many common factors among these accidents were discovered. These common factors included: preoccupation with minor technical problems, inadequate leadership, failure to delegate tasks and assign responsibilities, failure to set priorities, inadequate monitoring, failure to utilize available data, and failure to communicate intent and plans. The National Transportation Safety Board (NTSB) estimates that "human factors" contribute to 70% to 80% of airplane crashes.

Flight crew research and technological advances have been the major forces behind the changes in the airline interview process.

Out of this research comes the strong conclusion that communication and working as part of a team may do more to ensure a safe flight than an individual's technical skills. In addition, an airline pilot is now expected to play more of a public relations role which requires interaction with passengers whenever possible. For these reasons, in addition to the highly competitive atmosphere, it is no longer enough to simply be a technically competent aviator.

The interviewing process reflects this new outlook. And, viewed objectively, this new approach makes sense.

THE INTERVIEW PROCESS

In today's interview process there is still extensive review and critique of a pilot's technical capabilities. Comparatively, however, technical knowledge and skills are fairly easy to rate. After a review of training records and logbooks, a simulator ride, and a technical oral exam, a pilot's technical skill level is easily established.

To become familiar with an applicant's personality and attitude is not so easy. Mix in the fact that time is limited, and the result is an interview process filled with in-depth, pointed questions. The pilot interviewer must answer to his, and the airline's, satisfaction many questions:

- Will this individual speak up when necessary?

- Will this individual resolve conflicts quickly and in a mature and professional manner?

- Does this person have the ability to take criticism, and give criticism constructively?

- Will this person make an effective captain?

- Does this individual have strong academic abilities?

- Would I feel comfortable putting my family on a plane flown by this individual?

There is no simulator ride which can answer these questions. The answers are found only in face-to-face discussions and a critique of how an individual has handled himself in the past.

To make a fair assessment the interviewer uses every available source of information. They listen carefully to how you describe various experiences, question you further if they perceive a problem, critique your physical presentation, watch the way you interact with those around you, review your career progression and academic achievements, and ask for a mountain of documentation.

"Cockpit resource management is the effective utilization of all available resources - hardware, software, and liveware - to achieve safe, efficient flight operations. All crewmembers have resources available to them, and all have resource management responsibilities. Because of the unique role of the captain in providing leadership and command functions, he has more of the burden for effective personnel management than the other crewmembers. However, effective interpersonal skills are required of all people in the system."

From a speech by John K. Lauber, Ph.D., National Transportation Safety Board

To fully appreciate how seriously the airlines take this approach one need look no further than the introduction of Cockpit Resource Management (see sidebar) into the airline pilot training curriculum. The airlines provide this extensive training to help enhance a pilot's communication skills within the cockpit. From a purely monetary standpoint, it makes a great deal of sense to HIRE pilots who come to the cockpit with some innate abilities in these areas!

THE BOTTOM LINE

The bottom line is simple: if you are not prepared to fully share information about all areas of your background and experience the only decision that can be made is a negative one. And, to effectively answer these difficult questions one must take an organized, structured approach to self-critique.

Chapter 4

THE INTERVIEWER

To continue the logical process of preparing for an interview, in Chapters 4 and 5 we will:

- become familiar with the roles of the people involved in the process,

- gain an awareness of the most common interviewing mistakes.

THE ROLE In any field it is a major responsibility to recommend an individual for employment. A pilot interviewer has the added responsibility of recommending individuals who will be responsible for hundreds of thousands of lives over the length of a flying career. And this decision must be made after spending a relatively short time with each applicant. Added pressure on the interviewer comes from the fact that how well he does his job can be easily measured by the future success (or failure) of the applicants he recommends for employment.

The interviewer's job is a difficult and complex one. Because of the variety of concerns that must be addressed, the interviewer must be adept at uncovering the "real" person. It is their responsibility to discover if an applicant has the technical knowledge, communication skills, decision making abilities, leadership, and team orientation which will make him a positive influence in the cockpit. For these reasons an interviewer cannot "pussyfoot" around. He MUST ask pointed, probing questions of each applicant.

The approach an interviewer takes in an interview depends a great deal on his personality. Therefore, the tone of the interview can run the gamut from extreme formality to downright casual and from outright hostility to subtly intimidating.

THE STYLE OF THE INTERVIEW

It is important to remember that the average applicant tends to mirror the behavior of the interviewer. This poses no problem if the interviewing style is professional, formal, and friendly. However, problems abound when the style of the interviewer deviates from this formal approach. Some examples:

- **Casual, Friendly, Relaxed**

  To me the casual style of interviewing is the most effective for an interviewer and the most dangerous from the applicant's perspective.

  The interviewer leans back in his chair, sips coffee, and uses a conversational tone of voice and method of questioning: "I see you've been flying Lear jets for the past year—those are great aren't they?!" Suddenly, the applicant feels as though he is sitting with a friend talking airplanes. In this atmosphere the applicant is much more prone to offer information that is best left unoffered!

  Many years ago, I had a good friend who interviewed with a major carrier. He called after his interview full of high spirits. "It went great!" my friend reported, "I felt so comfortable with the interviewer. We even talked about that problem I had at work last year."

  Ouch! That problem had been resolved but the story did not put my otherwise tolerant friend in a very good light. I could only guess what else had been discussed. I groaned inwardly knowing the outcome would not be positive. He was not hired.

- **Aggressive, Intimidating**

  The interviewer starts the interview by surprising the applicant with a question like: "Although you graduated with a 3.5 GPA, I also noticed on your college transcripts that in your first two years your GPA was only 2.5. Can you explain this very poor performance to me?"

This type of questioning can put the unprepared applicant immediately on the defensive and may elicit a response that is equally aggressive: "Well, sir, I believe since I did—as you pointed out—end up with a 3.5 GPA that it is fairly clear to see that I was simply young. I also don't believe I would describe it as a 'very poor' performance."

Every response you give the interviewer is immediately put in the context of the position you will hold. Consequently, when you answer in an aggressive manner, the interviewer may feel as though you will not be able to maintain your professional demeanor even during minor confrontational situations (situations that occur daily on the line).

● Disinterested, Disorganized

This style does not happen often at the major carrier level; however, when encountered, it can be very disconcerting to the applicant.

The interviewer does not smile and the handshake seems insincere. He asks only those questions which are written down in front of him.

Or the interviewer may be disorganized. He can't find your resume, or a page of your application is missing. Perhaps he will think of something he needs to do in the middle of the interview and walk out of the office for several moments.

Both of these styles can give the applicant the feeling that the interview is being done just for "show" or perhaps to fill a daily quota.

The best approach to this style is, as always, a friendly and professional manner. Don't try to "break the ice" with a joke or too much small talk. Also, if the interview is interrupted remember what topic you were discussing. Many times the interviewer will come back to the interview and say "What were we talking about?" They usually know, but are looking to see if you were paying attention!

• Mixed Bag

I remembered our conversation about the different styles and just told myself it was all part of the plan!

It is not uncommon for an interview to begin in one tone (casual) and, out of the blue, change to a different tone (aggressive). At one particular airline the interviewing process includes several one-on-one interviews. An applicant may meet first with a personnel interviewer, then move to a meeting with a captain, and finally ending with a chief pilot.

A client called shortly after going through this process to tell me that he had encountered every type of style possible! "I felt totally at ease with the personnel interviewer and the first pilot with whom I interviewed. In fact, I felt so good I was expecting to be invited to someone's house for dinner! But, when I walked into the final interview with the chief pilot, the whole tone of the conversation changed. The way he asked me questions made me feel like he didn't believe anything I said. I started to feel like I had really messed up and had somehow done something wrong. Then I remembered our conversation about the different styles and just told myself it was all part of the plan! It was amazing but I began to relax after that and just kept right on answering his questions as best I could. By the end of the interview he was much friendlier and I felt as though he approved of me." He was hired.

Although the style can vary greatly interviewers are looking for the same information. It is imperative that you not get caught in the trap of taking the interviewer's approach personally! And, I must re-emphasize, do not attempt to "joke" an interviewer out of what you perceive to be a bad, or sad, mood! Comments such as, "Smile, it can't be that bad" usually only serve to annoy an individual.

No matter what style or groups of styles you encounter, always keep in mind, "They are not approaching me this way because they like/dislike me—they are simply doing their job." It is important to never forget where you are—IN AN INTERVIEW. If you keep this thought in mind you will find it much easier to maintain your friendly, even, and professional demeanor.

Chapter 5

THE APPLICANT

RESPONSIBILITIES

In a perfect world the interviewer would be able to spend two or three days learning all about you. But, the reality is that you will have a very limited amount of time together. For this reason you must understand your role in the interview.

- Be yourself!

As you go through the application and interview process you will discover a great many well-meaning souls who will give you all kinds of "sure-fire" advice on how to interview. Although I always encourage my clients to de-brief those individuals who have been through a specific airline process, it is important to remember that what works for one person will not necessarily net the same result for you.

I remember one individual I met with after an ill-fated interview. He was attempting to discover what had gone wrong. As we discussed his interview he mentioned that a friend of his suggested he start out the interview by slipping in an aviation joke. He took his friend's advice, but unfortunately no one laughed. Needless to say it was downhill from there.

What works for one person will not necessarily work for you.

Another potential client came to me and said, "I have three interviews in a row: American, Delta, and United. I want you to help me be an American pilot this week, a Delta pilot next week, and a United pilot next month." I pointed out that by taking that approach he was going to confuse himself. When he interviewed with an airline that was a great match with his true personality, he was going to be working so hard trying to be what he THOUGHT that airline wanted that his true personality would be hidden. "Besides," I explained, "these interviewers are good at spotting fakes." He finally agreed, dropped that approach, and was ultimately hired by his first choice airline.

If you are telling the truth you will be believed!

In another situation I met with a client who had already sent in his paperwork to his first choice airline. On the application under the question "How many days have you been absent from work or school in the last twelve months?" he had listed four times. This concerned me and I questioned him on it. He told me that he really had never been late or called in sick; however, a friend of his had told him if he listed no sick days the interviewer wouldn't believe him! By listening to unknowledgeable friends my client had added another problem area he would have to discuss!

If you are telling the truth you will be believed!

So, yes, learn about the format of the interview and what types of questions others were asked. But, when it comes to how to act during an interview—relax, be honest, and just be yourself!

- ● Be a Good "Information Giver."

It is YOUR responsibility to help the interviewer to get to know you. It is NOT necessarily the interviewer's responsibility to drag information out of you.

How do you become a good "information giver?"

It is quite straightforward. You must provide specific examples which clearly show how you handle yourself in various situations. The mistake many applicants make is they tend to **philosophize** their answers instead of being **specific.**

 For example, a corporate pilot is asked: "Tell me about a work problem you had and explain how you handled it."
The philosophical answer:
"Well, I feel the best way to handle a work problem is to approach it with a sense of humor and a sense of urgency."

 Versus the "information giver" answer:
"I remember a trip I flew when I was a corporate pilot. I was responsible for flying two businessmen around the country to a series of business meetings. Unfortunately, on our next to the last

leg home, we had to make an unscheduled stop at a small FBO in Iowa due to a mechanical problem. . ." You would then go on to describe how you got the airplane fixed, or how you arranged to get those businessmen home in time for their next meeting.

By describing a personal situation, something that happened TO YOU, you will help the interviewer gain insight into how you approach problems and handle conflicts. He will start to know the REAL you.

COMMON MISTAKES

• Not Listening

Several years ago I met a pilot interviewer at a friend's barbecue. When she learned the nature of my business she began to talk about some of the problems she saw on a daily basis. "I interviewed a very able gentleman today. He had great answers," she smiled, "unfortunately his answers had nothing to do with the questions I was asking!" Ah, I thought, the guy was not a good listener.

There will be subtle differences in questions that could cause you to answer incorrectly if you are not listening carefully. "What makes a good pilot?" should elicit a different response than "What makes a good captain?"

Subtle differences in questions could cause you to answer incorrectly if you are not listening carefully.

Too many people believe they know what the question is going to be just by hearing the first few words of the sentence. Instead of listening to the whole question they begin to plan their answer. This is a BIG mistake.

One way to avoid this problem is by what you are doing right now—preparing. Another way is to take a few seconds to replay the question in your mind before answering. This will help you make sure you heard the question correctly. A few seconds of silence will not cause the interviewer any concern, especially if your answer is thoughtful.

• Not Sharing Your Attention

If you are being interviewed by two or more people, make sure you acknowledge them all on an equal basis.

A common situation is to be interviewed by a pilot and a representative from Personnel. Perhaps because an applicant relates more to the pilot there is often a tendency to fixate on the pilot and direct all responses to him. This causes the Personnel representative to feel ignored. Not only is this rude, it does not say much for the applicant's communication and team orientation skills!

Remember, any interviewer can give you negative marks!

• Being Afraid of Silence

Silence during an interview can cause almost physical pain to the applicant. Every second of silence can seem like an eternity.

I teach my clients how to cope with silence during an interview by asking them this question: "When is a pilot most likely to make a mistake?" After careful consideration, the answer I receive is always the same, "When they move too quickly." Exactly!

Allow yourself a moment or two to make sure you are on the right track.

Making a decision too quickly can cause the wrong switch to be flipped, the wrong button to be pushed, the wrong command to be given. Even in times of extreme stress (perhaps most importantly in times of extreme stress) it is critical that a pilot allow his mind a second or two to make sure the problem is clear and the initial steps he is taking are correct.

The same holds true during an interview. Interviewers are not looking for people who say the first thing that enters their mind, regardless of the content. They are not interested in listening to a lot of pretty, meaningless words. Interviewers are interested in the thoughts and ideas behind the words.

CAUTION: Obviously, if you are asked "Have you ever been investigated by the FAA?" you are not going to take a few seconds to think the answer through! Point blank "yes" or "no" questions (Did you graduate from college? Have you ever failed a checkride?) need to be answered promptly and without hesitation.

Interviewers understand that sometimes a thoughtful answer needs some coaxing and some organization. So, if you need a moment to think about how you want to answer a question, do not be afraid to allow yourself some quiet thinking time! Remember, thoughtful silence from an applicant is not a source of concern for the interviewer, especially when they are rewarded with a clear, concise answer!

What about silence from the interviewer? If you have given what you feel is a thoughtful answer and the interviewer remains silent, don't take that as a sign that the interviewer doesn't understand or needs more information. Perhaps he is just writing down some comments or taking a moment to organize his next question. If the interviewer wants more information from you, he will ask for it.

• Venting Personal Frustrations

Although you are in the interview to talk about yourself, now is not the time to philosophize about how things **should** have gone in your life. It is not that interviewers are unsympathetic, but we have all had our share of hard times. The purpose of the interview is for you to give information, not search for sympathy.

If you are asked about a difficult situation ("Why were you fired from this job?"), be professional and factual in your answers. Do not use this an an opportunity to talk about what you believe SHOULD have happened ("My boss just didn't like me, I should have been given another chance").

Although you do not want to dwell on difficult situations, do not go overboard and try to make your life appear as though you have never encountered difficult decisions, problems, or conflicts. This type of presentation is unrealistic, unbelievable, and may be perceived as "canned."

It is important to leave the interviewer with the impression of, "Yes, it was a difficult time/terrible situation, this is how I handled myself, and what I learned from the situation. But, that is behind me and I am moving forward."

• Not Being Professional

All the people you come in contact with are professionals within their field. Any hint of rudeness on your part will not be tolerated. In addition, this is not the time to look for special favors or to ask for special treatment.

✈ *I heard about one applicant who, after his interview, asked the receptionist to re-write his airline pass so he could go to his high school reunion in another city. The receptionist explained that re-writing the ticket was against the rules. The applicant became incensed and asked to speak to the receptionist's supervisor. (Gee, I wonder if he got hired?)*

Always remember where you are and why you are there. Because the aviation community is somewhat close knit, it is not uncommon to bump into a friend or acquaintance in the airline's offices while you are waiting for your interview. It is easy to slip into unsuitable conversations. Be careful of reminiscing, discussing the problems of the aviation industry, or bemoaning the state of the job market. Personally, I would not even want to be a part of a group listening to such conversations. Once again, always remember where you are (at a very competitive interview) and why you are there (to get a great job!), and do not let outside circumstances push you off track or allow you to lose your focus!

• Joking

I have met very few people who can carry off a joke under the stress of an interview. Never plan to tell a joke or try to 'lighten up' the interview. I had one client who, throughout the course of our work together, kept asking me if it was OK to joke about this or all right to interject a funny quote about that. My answer was continually "No." However, it was obvious his feeling continued to be that trying to be funny would be a plus in the interview. As I suspected, during his interview he was overcome with the desire to tell a joke, the joke fell flat, the interviewer appeared mildly insulted, and my client was embarrassed. (He was not hired. I suspect he tried more than one joke.)

Use your smile often. This advice does not mean that you shouldn't show a sense of humor! If something funny is said (either by the interviewer or, ACCIDENTALLY, by you) smile or laugh! Also, because you want to appear approachable and friendly, use your smile often.

● Trying to Lead the Interview

To be completely prepared you should have many stories to share with the interviewer that will clearly show how you handle yourself in various situations. However, it is human nature to have a couple of "really good" stories that you want to tell!

Surprise! The interviewer just isn't cooperating. The questions being asked just don't lend themselves to telling these "really good" stories!

Do not become so fixated on wanting to tell these stories that you decide, "Oh, well, this doesn't really answer the question—but, I'm going to tell it anyway!" If the story doesn't clearly answer the question, what does that say about your ability to LISTEN?

In addition, if you tell stories that are not applicable to the questions, the impression might be that you are trying to lead the interview.

It is much more to your advantage to answer the questions with applicable responses. In this way the interviewer will feel that you are working with them, not just trying to complete your own agenda.

- Berating / Anticipating

There are two areas where it is very easy to lose your train of thought.

Berating Yourself: You are not going to have perfect interview! You will say something that you wish you hadn't, or perhaps you will give the wrong answer to a technical question. When this occurs don't allow yourself to waste valuable time worrying about it! Recognize the error and say to yourself, "I'll get mad at myself LATER!" (If you answer a *technical* question incorrectly, and realize your mistake later in the interview, it is perfectly acceptable to say, "Pardon me, I was incorrect on the question concerning the fuel dump procedure, the correct answer is ...")

Live second-by-second
in the interview.
LISTEN
REPLAY
DECIDE

Anticipating Questions: Even though this book is based on NOT preparing question-by-question, it is difficult not to review the list of questions that are available through the "applicant grapevine." Intense review of those questions makes it easy to feel as though you know what the question is going to be, even before the interviewer finishes asking it! The interviewer says: "Tell me about a conflict you had with a captain..." While you are thinking to yourself, "Oh, I know that one!" the interviewer finishes the question with, "...that you have been unable to resolve." If the situation you talk about doesn't answer the question exactly—you will lose points!

To avoid anticipating questions, live second-by-second in the interview. Listen to the question, replay it in your mind, THEN decide upon an applicable answer.

- Trying to argue the unarguable

If you have made a mistake, admit it! Show that you do accept responsibility for your actions. Don't try to argue your way out of it in the interview by saying such things as you didn't know the rules, there were extenuating circumstances, everyone else was doing it, etc.

One client discussed a situation where as F/O he allowed a captain to not complete checklists. I asked him, "Do you believe that is safe?"

Instead of saying, "No. I handled the situation incorrectly. I know now there are many things I could have done to not place myself in that situation," he said, "Well, not AS safe."

I once again asked him for a "yes" or "no" answer. He continued to avoid answering directly and replied, "Not as safe, but it was ok in this situation." I then asked if he frequently decided what rules and regulations were not important to follow?

He never fully answered the question and consistently evaded responsibility. The impression left on an interviewer would be of a person who is argumentative, unwilling to accept responsibility, and only follows the rules when it fits his needs.

● Not being focused

I came out to meet my client, shook his hand and asked him to follow me back to my office. When I reached my office I realized he was not with me. I retraced my steps back to the waiting room and found him filling his coffee cup and asking the receptionist for more sugar. I felt a little surge of irritation. For the first half hour of our consultation he was completely unfocused. He eventually calmed down and did fairly well. However, had it been the real interview, it would have been too late to repair the damage his initial behavior had caused.

Maintain your focus on the interviewer and the task at hand!

● Having others make arrangements for you

It is always best for YOU to make all your interview arrangements with the airline. Obviously, sometimes that is not possible and you must depend on someone else to do it for you. In this case, it is imperative that you brief them as to correct etiquette. Make sure they understand that any rude or uncompromising behavior could have a direct effect on you.

- ## Not having the correct paperwork

The people making the hiring decision look carefully at an applicant's paperwork. Poor paperwork presentation says, "This applicant does not care." Remember, the paperwork package you initially present to the company will follow you through the whole interviewing process.

 A veteran pilot called my office one afternoon and requested that I review his paperwork. The airline he was applying to kept sending it back and he simply could not figure out the problem. After faxing me the paperwork, the very first page showed the problem. He had filled out a GROUND SERVICE application.

Before sending off any paperwork you must ask yourself, "If I were looking at this paperwork for the first time how would I feel about the person who sent it?" Is it neat? Have the directions been followed? Is the grammar and spelling correct? Is the typing or printing neat? Have all the questions been answered clearly and completely?

Have a friend review your entire package before sending it to the airline. After spending hours and hours working on an application and resume, it is difficult to pick up even glaring errors (as my "ground service" pilot found out!).

Also, HIRE A PROFESSIONAL to type your resume, application, and cover letters. It is worth it for the professional appearance it will give to your paperwork.

- ## Poor physical presentation

When you mention physical presentation people usually think of how someone dresses. However, physical presentation also includes body language, eye contact, your state of health, and your grooming. Now is the time to take a honest look at the kind of overall impression you give.

● Poor technical preparation

Do not assume that just because you have thousands of hours of flight time, no violations, and an excellent training record that you will not be asked to show your technical knowledge.

It is very important that you approach the technical side of the interview as you would a proficiency check, an upgrade checkride, or an FAA examination.

I met with an individual who had been a pilot instructor in the military. As we talked about one of his past interviews I asked him how he felt he had done on the technical portion.

"Well," he replied, "I missed 3 or 4 questions (out of 9 or 10) but they must know I have solid technical knowledge, I was an instructor!"

No, an interviewer will never assume anything of the sort. In fact, the interviewer was probably surprised that a past pilot instructor would do poorly in the technical interview. This pilot was not offered a position.

Notes

Chapter 6

SELF-EVALUATION
Discovering Your Stories

The best way to successfully communicate your strengths, aptitudes, experience, and desire to the interviewer is to provide specific, personal examples in response to questions. I call these personal examples "stories."

There are two goals in these self-evaluation exercises:

1. **To discover your stories**. The exercises will help you remember specific conflicts, work and personal decisions/problems, celebrations, and crises that you have encountered during your lifetime.

2. **To dissect your stories**. The exercises will help you dissect your stories and assist you in understanding how you handled the situations and what you learned from them.

Almost every client that has gone through my program has commented that these self-evaluation exercises were instrumental in helping them to recall, understand, develop and deliver their stories. Because of these consistent remarks, these exercises are the foundation of my pilot interview preparation program.

During these exercises it is important to remember that we are all different. This is not the time to begin comparing yourself with other applicants. Use this preparation process to recognize all the strengths you possess and to become comfortable in discussing your weaknesses.

Each person will have a different opinion on the difficulty of these exercises. Some will find it fairly easy to remember situations and within two days will have a basketful of stories to tell. Others may have to spend two or three weeks reviewing this worksheet before they feel comfortable and ready.

Remember, no matter what category you find yourself in, given enough time you will remember many appropriate stories!

Before You Begin

The goal of the following exercises is to have a complete understanding of the subject of the interview: *you*.

To reach this understanding it is necessary to thoroughly critique your approach towards problems and situations in all areas of your life. How do you handle conflicts? What do you do when a superior makes a decision you are uncomfortable with? How do you critique a subordinate? What is your approach towards solving problems? Only when you are completely comfortable in your understanding of your personal approaches will you be able to sit down and make your points clearly to a total stranger. If this sounds like a tall order, don't fret too much. By following the suggestions in this book you will be pleasantly surprised at how much easier and more specific your answers to the interviewer's questions will be!

● Today's Airline Pilot

In addition to being knowledgeable about today's sophisticated interviewing process, a pilot applicant must be aware of the changing face of today's airline pilot.

For years we have known that, although important, strong "stick and rudder" skills were not enough to reach the pinnacle of the pilot profession: the major airline cockpit. For many years the pilot interviewing process has focused on areas that are separate from the *physical* act of using the stick and rudder: leadership, team orientation, decision making, attitude, communication, and learning ability.

It is now important to show a professional approach in these areas from another perspective: customer service.

Today's airline pilot must be as aware of their attitude, communication, decision-making, leadership, and team orientation in the customer service arena as they are in the cockpit and employee relations arena!

I worked with a client who was telling me about a conflict with his co-pilot. The disagreement involved a passenger wanting to stow a large piece of luggage in the cabin because the luggage was "fragile." This, as my captain client stated, was against company policy and a clear safety issue. "Fine", I thought to myself, "logical and appropriate." However, his next comment raised my antenna, "I told my copilot, 'Listen, every passengers luggage is 'fragile.' The passengers luggage is *not* my problem."

Uh-oh! This client was coming across as completely oblivious to the importance of customer service. In today's competitive business atmosphere customer service is becoming a top priority in maintaining customer share. A "not my problem" approach is not the type of attitude an airline would want to hire.

Be aware that the interviewer is listening intently to not only how you interact with your co-workers but also how you relate to passengers.

● Talk Pilot?

When searching for your stories the primary field of investigation should be your flying experiences.

However, as I mentioned in the Introduction, because of the incredible "gouge" available within the pilot community interviewers are constantly reviewing better ways to gauge an applicant's history. A result of this fact is that many interviewers are now interested not only in how you handle yourself when in a flying situation, but also how you handle yourself on the ground.

It is not unusual for an interviewer to ask a question such as, "Tell me about a time you failed as a leader *outside* the cockpit." These types of questions require self-evaluation in other areas of your life other than flying.

For example a civilian pilot might discuss a situation that occurred when he managed the aircraft scheduling for a flight school, or perhaps when he was in charge of a day-long conference. A military pilot might look to his experience as the Standards and Evaluation Officer for an applicable story or any situation within his non-flying officer experience.

Please don't get confused. Unless specifically requested to discuss a non-flying situation your stories should still encompass your flying. However, do not ignore your non-flying experiences. In order to have a well-rounded understanding of your personal approach you must spend as much time reviewing your non-flying experiences in order to be ready for those "on the ground" questions!

● Understand the Question – Think Like an Interviewer

Another way to better understand the interviewing process, and thus find your stories easier, is to think like an interviewer. You need to ask yourself: *Why* is the interviewer asking that question? *What* is the interviewer trying to learn? For example:

Question: Tell me about a conflict you have had with a captain. Interviewer's Reasoning: *What* type of conflicts, with superiors, does this person encounter? *How* do they handle people with whom they are in conflict? Does this person have the ability to raise their concerns to a person who is in a position of authority?

Question: Tell me about a time you were assertive in the cockpit. IR: *What* type of situations does this person feel requires assertiveness? *How* do they approach demonstrating assertiveness?

Question: Tell me about a policy you disagreed with. What did you do?
IR: *What* type of policies does this person disagree with? *How* does this person approach voicing displeasure or disagreement? *How* does this person respond if the policy remains standing?

Become adept at uncovering the reasoning behind a question by *thinking like an interviewer.* This will make it much easier for you to answer a question that perhaps catches you off guard.

● People Review

Spend some time thinking about people. Review all the captains, first officers, chief pilots, bosses, students, instructors, fellow pilots, etc., you have worked with through your lifetime.

As you remember these individuals one-by-one you will become flooded with memories. "Oh, I haven't thought about Matt for years. I remember the day we had that mechanical coupled with the thunderstorms..." By thinking about the time spent with Matt you may remember a story that will help you answer a question during your interview. In this instance perhaps you and Matt had a disagreement about the routing for the trip (story for question: a conflict with a co-worker), or the mechanical problem was one you had never seen before (a difficult technical problem you had and how you handled it.).

DECISION MAKING ABILITY

Decision making ability is an underlying theme during the entire interviewing process.

How well an airline runs depends heavily on the decisions that are made by its on-the-scene employees. Nowhere is this more true than in the cockpit. Pilots are called upon to make decisions that affect safety, on-time schedule, passenger comfort, etc. Sometimes the pilot has the luxury of having the time to work through the problem, but often the decision needs to be made in a split second. Airlines want pilots who exhibit a strong ability to work through problems logically while taking into consideration factors of safety, comfort, and expense.

- **ASK YOURSELF**—Decision Making

What are some of the hardest decisions I have ever had to make?

Leaving RE FLIGHT school LGW

What process did I go through to arrive at my final decision?

Long term decision - focus on long term

What is the biggest mistake I have ever made? What did I learn from that mistake? *Not starting to fly sooner*

1) Make sure info is correct; consider the source
3) Believe in myself

What split-second decisions have I had to make? How did I make them? (e.g., emergency situations) *Last Con Runway change When in doubt; no!*

If I have a long-term decision to make, what process do I use to make this decision? (e.g., anticipated bad weather for a four-day trip) *Gather info*

• SAMPLE QUESTIONS—Decision Making

Educational Background

Why did you choose this major?

Gts

How did you pay for school?

Why did you choose that college?

*"What **did** you do **WHEN**…" questions require a specific example from your background.*
*"What **would** you do **IF**…" questions require you to provide an example of your thought process should you encounter such a situation in the future.*

How did you attain your flight training? How did you pay for it?

Work Situations

Tell me about a work problem and how you handled it.

Tell me about a mistake you made in the cockpit.

High mins captain (RVR all three)

Tell me about a conflict you had with a supervisor and how you handled it.

What were your reasons for leaving your past employers?

Situational Questions

What would you do if a captain made a decision you did not agree with?

What would you do if your Captain was asking questions about your personal life?

Tell him

Tell me about a time someone tried to get you to do something you were NOT comfortable doing.

COMMUNICATION

Airlines are looking for individuals who understand the importance of keeping the lines of communication open and flowing no matter what the situation or personalities involved. Communication is paramount during times of conflict and stress.

An excellent way to gauge an individual's ability to communicate is to ask questions about problems at work or conflicts with co-workers and supervisors.

The interviewer will be asking himself, "Do I feel confident that this individual possesses the ability to speak up when necessary? Do I feel as though this individual can give AND TAKE constructive criticism professionally? Does this individual have the ability to articulate his thoughts and ideas clearly? Does this individual have the sensitivity and compassion to approach a co-worker who seems distraught or in need of assistance?

● ASK YOURSELF—Communication

What conflicts (large or small) have I had with co-workers? (Misunderstandings about scheduling, disagreement about how to handle a customer, you heard from a friend that a co-worker spoke ill of you, basic personality conflicts, etc.)

What specific steps did I take to handle the conflicts?

How were the conflicts finally resolved?

Have I ever had a conflict with a superior or supervisor? What steps did I take to handle the conflict? What was the resolution? *Captain ran off the start ✓ last during taxi: (it is on tape)*

Were there ever any conflicts that I was never able to fully resolve? What were the reasons for my inability to resolve this conflict? How would I handle the conflict differently?

Have I ever found myself stuck in the middle of a conflict between two other people? What did I do?

Was I ever the cause of a problem at work? How did I resolve the problem?

In general, what steps do I take when I find myself involved in a conflict with a co-worker/supervisor/superior?
Look again at situation - more closely

How would my peers/supervisors describe me?
Analytical, thoughtful; considerate easy to get along with

How would my family describe me?

● SAMPLE QUESTIONS—Communication

Tell me about a conflict you have had with a supervisor.
Bod mag

Have you ever disagreed with a decision made by your captain?

How did you handle the situation? *listen to Caption - discussed on ground: unless imediatly safety related*

Have you ever flown with someone you felt was unsafe? What did you do?

HINT: *If an individual has trouble articulating how others would describe him—it may appear that the individual doesn't care, or has never asked for others' critique.*

Have you ever had to apologize to a co-worker?

Tell me about a problem you caused. How did you handle it?

Call in sick

Have you ever been counseled at work?

LEADERSHIP

Airlines are looking for CAPTAINS not lifetime co-pilots or second officers. However, the co-pilots and second officers must possess the ability to speak up when the situation warrants. For this reason airlines are keenly interested in the leadership abilities and potential for leadership in their candidates.

• ASK YOURSELF—Leadership

What leadership roles have I held during my lifetime? List them. (Think chronologically beginning with high school.)

Real Estate / Rowing
lead by example: earn respect; not demand it

Remember, airlines are looking for CAPTAINS.

While in these various roles what problems did I encounter? (i.e., personnel conflicts within the organization, differences of opinion on the focus of the group, fund raising shortages, low membership roster, low morale within the organization, etc.)

How did I handle these situations?

What did I learn from each new situation?

SERVICE

What mistakes have I made while in a leadership role? What did I learn from these mistakes?

RE: my way only
listen more / listen better

Has my style of leadership changed over the years? Why has it changed? *more relaxed*

What adjectives would describe my leadership style?

Decisive, team oriented; does his homework

Have I ever had to take on a leadership role unexpectedly? What were the circumstances? What was the outcome? What did I learn from that experience?

● SAMPLE QUESTIONS—Leadership

What leadership roles have you held during your lifetime?

Of what leadership role are you most proud?

Eng Yds (Jan 5th)

How would you describe your leadership style?

SERVICE

Has your style of leadership changed over the years?

Where have you failed in a leadership role? What did you learn from this experience?

Not gotten through to on FO
about why I wanted something done *Dvve for*
(direct when able) *purpose*

TEAM ORIENTATION

Although there is a definite leadership hierarchy the cockpit is also a team oriented atmosphere. If the individuals in the cockpit do not work together lives could be lost.

● ASK YOURSELF—Team Orientation

When have I been a part of a team (e.g., community service, sports, committees, etc.)? List these memberships.

Have I ever been involved in team problem solving (e.g., in-flight emergency or a mechanical problem, planning a workshop or lecture, member of a productivity committee at work, etc.)?

What problems have I had working as a part of a team (conflicts with other members, team goals not met)? What did I learn from these situations?

Have I been involved in emergency situations where we solved the problem by working as a team (e.g., flying emergencies, medical emergencies, family emergencies)?

Was I ever the individual who came up with a solution while working as a part of the team? How did I suggest this solution? Was it accepted as the final solution? Why or why not?

Tell me about a problem you helped solve through group problem solving.

What don't you like about working as a part of a team?

Weaker team members Slm

Did you ever disagree with a decision made by a captain (or supervisor)? How did you handle it?

Has a captain ever disagreed with a decision you made? How did you handle it?

ATTITUDE

An employee with a positive attitude is invaluable to any employer. In the cockpit it can make dealing with weather, mechanical delays, and passenger problems less stressful for everyone. A positive attitude lays the groundwork for good communication and positive team interaction.

Asking questions about problem areas is a great way to gauge someone's true attitude. Does the individual take responsibility for their mistakes, or do they make excuses? Does the individual answer the question in a straightforward way or does he use the question as a forum to discuss how he was treated poorly? How does this individual describe past employers and co-workers?

● ASK YOURSELF—Attitude

What difficulties have I faced during my lifetime (e.g., unable to find employment or being furloughed, illness in the family, unable to fund college, etc.)? How did I get through these difficult times? What specific steps did I take to solve these problems?

Have I ever been in a situation where my behavior caused problems (work, personal)? What did I learn from those situations?

How would I describe my past jobs and employers?

● IF APPLICABLE—Attitude

Why was I fired? What did I learn from that experience?

Why were my grades so poor in college?

Why did I flunk that checkride?

- SAMPLE QUESTIONS—Attitude

What has been the most difficult decision you have ever had to make? *flight school*

Tell me why you received a D in algebra.

Why were you fired from your college job?

Why have you been out of work for a year?

Why did you fail that checkride?

How did you like your last/first/present job? Why did you leave?

LEARNING ABILITY

As a professional pilot you will be called upon to use your training on a daily basis. For these reasons a potential employer will be looking for pilot applicants with a proven, strong ability to grasp and retain new ideas quickly and completely. It is not financially sound to hire an individual who may require additional training.

Learning abilities can also be gauged through a technical oral exam, a simulator ride, and a review of past academic records.

The interviewer will also be interested in the applicant's ability to learn lessons in his personal life. Does he learn from his mistakes or does he continue to make the same mistakes over and over?

● ASK YOURSELF—Learning

Looking over my past academic experiences why have I excelled/done poorly?

How do I study?

● SAMPLE QUESTIONS—Learning

Why did you not graduate from college?

Why were your grades so poor in college?

Why did it take you so long to graduate from college?

Why didn't you upgrade when first possible?

Why do you have two speeding tickets?

Why have you had three jobs in four years?

Telling Your Story

Now that you have gathered your stories it is time to learn how to effectively deliver those stories.

Begin by organizing each story into 3 parts: a beginning, a middle, and an end. The next step is to decide what information is important to mention under each part.

You have two minutes to tell your story.

By following these two basic guidelines you will discover that your "story telling" becomes more organized and more complete while at the same time taking less time to tell. As a general rule you should attempt to complete each story in two minutes or less. (Stop reading and time two minutes. It's a LONG time!)

THE BEGINNING

PURPOSE: To set the scene

The circumstances (time, place, your experience level) surrounding the story must be clear to the interviewer. Many times, because you are so familiar with the situation, you may inadvertently leave out pertinent information.

For instance, a retired major in the air force is asked to give an example of a specific work problem and how he handled it:

The unprepared applicant might begin:
"When I was in the military I was on a mission and a problem developed. . ."

Perhaps this individual had a 15 year military career. Did this problem develop when he was a lieutenant or a major? We can't tell from his statement.

The prepared applicant would state:
"When I was a MAJOR in the AIR FORCE I was a CO-PILOT on a two-week mission to CENTRAL AMERICA and a week into the trip a problem developed..."

This second example shows the time (towards the end of his career), place (two week mission to Central America) experience level (co-pilot).

- More examples of clearly setting the scene:

> When I was a flight instructor. . . versus When I was a new flight instructor working with my first student. . .
>
> When I was in college. . .versus It was the beginning of my junior year in college. . .
>
> When I was in flight training. . . versus When I was completing my Multi-Engine instructor rating. . .

THE MIDDLE

PURPOSE: To provide only the events that are necessary to understand the story. To provide the events in a chronological order.

CAUTION: Don't use real names when telling a story. It's a small world, and perhaps an individual in one of your stories is interviewing with the same interviewer next week.

We have all listened to poor storytellers recounting an experience. Often the reason they are poor storytellers is that they leave out information or fail to tell the story in an organized manner. They verbally jump around in the story trying vainly to fill in the blanks in a failing attempt to explain their experience more clearly. The listener becomes confused, can't follow the storyteller's train of thought and, after a while tires of even trying!

One of my clients, a flight instructor, told me about a conflict he had with a co-worker:
"It was my second week on the job and the gentleman who was the senior flight instructor returned from vacation. You know, we became really good friends after this misunderstanding, but boy he was really upset at the beginning! Anyway, he had been on vacation and when he returned many of the new students had been given to me. You know, I didn't even know there was a problem but it turns out the scheduler was new and didn't understand the process of signing up new students. ANYWAY, he came back from vacation and thought that I had purposely taken these students..."

This client set the scene correctly, but jumped to the end of the story. He then repeated himself and jumped to the middle of the story. Not only was I confused, he confused himself as well!

Give the highlights of the story, and keep the events in a chronological order.

Mention only the IMPORTANT events. Provide them in the order they occurred:

"It was my second week as a flight instructor. Tom, the senior flight instructor, had just returned from vacation. We had not yet met. While he had been on vacation I had been given three new students. Tom checked the schedule and became very upset when he saw I had acquired so many new students. He came to me, very agitated, and asked me what I thought I was doing. I remember saying, "Hold on, there's been some mistake, I simply was taking those students I had been assigned." I suggested we go visit the scheduler together. We did and immediately discovered the error. It turned out that I should only have been given one student, but the scheduler was also new and not familiar with the process. Tom took one of my new students and the third was given to another instructor. He apologized for coming at me so aggressively. We worked together for the next two years and became friends."

The format of this story clearly sets the scene, gives the listener the highlights of the story, and keeps the events in a chronological order. It is easy to follow, brief, and complete.

If the points you want to make are not clear to you, how will they ever be clear to the interviewer?

Another of my clients was trying to tell me about a work problem. He was only half way through after speaking for five minutes. At the six minute mark he stopped, blushed beet red, and said, "This story is so long, and now it's gotten so boring, I can't even remember what I was talking about!"

THE END

PURPOSE: To resolve any emotional conflict or technical problem that occurred during your story.

All stories need an ending. If you do not put an ending on your story, the interviewer will do it for you. And, since the interviewer will not assume anything positive, it will not be a happy ending.

I was working with a pilot who had over ten years of airline experience. During our mock interview I asked him to recount for me a situation where he had disagreed with a captain.

If you do not put an ending on your story, the interviewer will do it for you.

"I had been with the airline about a year and was flying with a captain I had never met before. I was flying the leg into Reagan Airport in D.C. Although new to the airline I had a great deal of experience flying in and out of this airport. On our initial approach I thought the altitude the captain gave me seemed wrong. I asked him if he would confirm. He immediately became defensive and said that he hadn't made a mistake. I responded that although he was probably right I would feel much more comfortable if he would check just to ease my mind. Grudgingly he made the call and discovered he was in error."

My client stopped the story there. In the few seconds we sat in silence I thought to myself, "Boy, I'll bet they didn't talk to each other for the rest of the trip!" (Which in turn made me think he must not be a very good communicator, team player, etc.)

Luckily, he quickly realized his mistake and gave me the ending of the story: "When we got on the ground I briefly thanked the captain for making the call. I then invited him to grab a bite to eat with me during our three hour wait and he accepted. We had a great time together the rest of the trip."

If he had not completed the story I, and an interviewer, would have had a completely different view of that situation. It would have been a negative story instead of a positive one!

SITUATIONAL QUESTIONS

Here is a concrete way to think about a situational question: The question you are asked is placed in your front yard, the final resolution to the question is on your roof. Obviously you can't jump from your front yard to the roof, you will need a ladder. Your thought process is that ladder.

Although the resolution of a situational question is important, perhaps even more important is the thought process you used to decide on a course of action which resulted in the final resolution of the situation.

"You are a co-pilot on the 737. The captain is flying. You have just received clearance for take-off. However the flight attendants have not yet completed their safety demonstration. The captain looks at you and says 'Let's go.' What do you do?"

The first applicant says:
"I wouldn't let him go."

The second applicant:
"My first inclination would be to think that the captain was not aware of the situation. I would inform him that the flight attendants had not yet completed their duties and taken their assigned seats. If he insisted on proceeding, I would then say something like, 'Sir, not only is that against all regulations, but if one of the flight attendants were to be injured they, the company, and the FAA would have every right to come after us both.' I would then offer to call the senior flight attendant to make sure he realizes that we are ready to go. The bottom line is we cannot begin our take-off roll until everyone is safely seated."

Now, BOTH applicants came up with the same resolution. But, as an interviewer, wouldn't you feel more comfortable with applicant #2's response? He gave you his thought process step-by-step.

• Visualize

Imagine for a moment you are taking an FAA oral. The examiner is sitting across the desk from you and asks: "What is the procedure for an engine-out?"

In order to not miss any steps in your response, you are probably envisioning the cockpit panel. You see yourself flipping the correct switches and following the appropriate checklists. Use this same approach with situational questions.

Listen carefully to the way the interviewer sets up the question. Then place yourself in that scene.

"As co-pilot on a 737 you have just taken off from Boston. Immediately after take-off the airport is closed due to a terrible snow storm. The captain is flying and you are still below 10,000 feet. The flight attendant knocks on the door and says there is a situation in the cabin he cannot control (medical emergency, fight, etc.). The captain looks at you and says 'We are going to go back and land at Boston.' What are you going to do?"

Before answering the question, place yourself in that co-pilot's seat, SEE the terrible snowstorm, HEAR the flight attendant knocking on the door. Then, with that scene in your mind, talk the interviewer through how you would approach solving the problem.

If your first step would be to tell the captain that landing is against all FAR's—tell the interviewer! If your second step would be to give suggestions of landing alternates—tell that to the interviewer, too!

Each step you offer is a rung in the ladder which will bring you closer to the final resolution. Answering in this specific manner will allow the interviewer to understand how you work through problems and conflicts.

Be aware that there is a danger in becoming too long-winded in answering situational questions. You should still strive to keep your answers under two minutes.

Addressing Problem Areas

Discussing one's faults and mistakes is, for almost everyone, an anxiety-producing part of an interview. However, areas of weakness or failure do not have to be overwhelmingly difficult to discuss.

It is important to remember that we all have faults. EVERYONE has personal situations they would rather not discuss. It makes no difference if the pilot is 20 years old with 200 hours of flight time, or 50 years old with 20,000 hours—all have "skeletons" in their closets. The severity of the problems may vary but the level of discomfort is the same—HIGH.

Beware of becoming irritated, frustrated, or defensive.

One of the worst mistakes you can make during an interview is to show irritation, frustration, or defensiveness towards the interviewer. These emotions usually surface when an individual is caught unprepared or unwilling to discuss a problem area. For these reasons, it is important to face those areas you would prefer never to discuss (or think about!) again. Through a thorough examination of past mistakes you will:

- know exactly what words you want to use when explaining the situation,

- be able to anticipate follow-up questions,

- be able to point out what you learned and how you improved, and

- ultimately discover the anticipation is far worse than the actual questioning!

Absolutes

First, let's look at two hard and fast, never-to-be-compromised rules you must follow when discussing problem areas.

1. Never lie.

The majority of pilot candidates would never consider lying in an interview.

However, when it comes to discussing problem areas many candidates are sometimes tempted to "alter" the circumstances of the problem or perhaps present the problem with a few "specifics" left out.

There is no problem area as damaging as being caught in a lie.

You will get points for being open and honest. But, if you are discovered in a lie, no matter how minor or innocuous it may seem, any chance of being considered for employment will be lost. The question that will immediately come to the interviewer's mind will be "If this individual has lied to us, even on a minor point, what else is he hiding?"

2. Take responsibility.

A mature individual takes responsibility for mistakes. A candidate who rationalizes a mistake will not be viewed as such an individual.

Several years ago I met with two clients in the same afternoon. As I reviewed their paperwork in advance, I discovered one candidate had a minor FAA violation. The other candidate had two traffic tickets. Although the traffic tickets were going to be difficult to explain, I felt the FAA violation would be far more damaging.

After meeting with these two candidates my outlook completely reversed.

The individual with the minor FAA violation came to our meeting prepared and ready to discuss the situation. He presented me with all the paperwork concerning the incident (FAA and NTSB reports and his written explanation of the incident to each agency). He remained calm, helpful, and professional during our 45 minute discussion.

Although the violation was still a problem, I felt confident the interviewer would give this individual every consideration. Happily, this turned out to be the case. The individual was questioned for almost an hour about the situation, the violation was thoroughly researched by the airline, and this individual was hired.

The second candidate, in sharp contrast to the first, refused to admit that the traffic tickets had been his fault. He pointed the finger at everyone but himself. Both tickets had been for speeding and he complained that there had been a speed trap and "lots of people got caught." His comments were: "That road shouldn't be 45 mph!" and, "The city just wants the money!" Although technically and educationally well qualified, this individual did not make it past the initial screening interview.

Not surprising!

When discussing a problem area, tell the complete story and accept responsibility for your actions.

During the Discussion of a Problem Area . . .

. . . Show Improvement

The individual with the FAA violation not only talked openly about the violation, he also made sure I knew that he had worked hard to improve. He pointed out that since the incident he had 10 years of excellent training reports, he had upgraded early and easily, and he had no more dealings with the FAA! He provided me with letters of recommendation from an FAA investigator and the employer he was working for at the time of the violation.

The candidate with the speeding tickets had received his last ticket two years prior to this interview. Had he taken responsibility for his actions and pointed out that he had had two years without a traffic violation, the interviewer may have been satisfied and thought no more of the situation.

• Examples of Showing Improvement

These examples are given for illustration only. It is common practice to be asked to document the specific reasons for your difficulties.

Poor college grades?

Mention that you have never failed a checkride and always scored 95% or above in your flight tests.

Failed a checkride?

Let the interviewer know that you went back the next day and passed with flying colors.

No college degree?

A college degree is becoming mandatory with the major carriers.

Focus on what you did during the time when many of your peers were attending college. Did you have to choose between flight training and college? Did your family need your assistance at that time? Do you have plans to complete your education?

A college degree is becoming mandatory with the major carriers. The lack of a degree will be a drawback. If at all possible, think about returning to school, even part-time, to complete your education.

Flunked out of college?

For this situation it is imperative that you show improvement in a learning arena.

If you returned to school and completed your degree, then failing the first time will not be a difficult problem to overcome IF you take responsibility for the failure.

If you flunked out of college and never returned now is a good time to do so. Excelling in a few classes will lessen the interviewer's concern about your learning skills and ability to set and reach goals.

. . . Provide documentation

If the problem area is documented by a public or private agency (FAA, driver's license bureau, the courts, college registrar's office, etc.) bring all applicable paperwork. Make copies of the originals to leave with the interviewer.

In the case of a flying situation, you may also present your explanation to the interviewer in written form.

● Examples Of Appropriate Documentation

Traffic tickets?

Take your most recent driving record (original and copies) to the interview. Take responsibility!

FAA violation?

You should make all applicable paperwork available to the interviewer including: the FAA report on the incident and any follow up letters, any NTSB reports, and your written statement to the FAA.

Fired from a job?

Collect letters of recommendation from all of your other employers. Although employers are only supposed to give out dates of employment, many times the tone of the recommendation will give away the true situation. Call the employer who fired you and ask what he will say when the airline calls or writes for a recommendation. A face-to-face meeting (or a phone call) may soften the past employer's outlook on your situation. At the very least, by investigating the situation you will know what you are up against.

Unusual Medical Background or Injury?

If you have any type of medical situation or past injury which may be viewed as unusual by the airline's medical department make sure you bring all applicable paperwork concerning the situation.

. . . Be aware of your body language

. . . Don't make the interviewer have to drag the information out of you.

When discussing problem areas body language becomes additionally important. It is imperative that you maintain good eye contact, that your voice is strong, and your hands and legs remain relaxed and quiet.

Interviewer: I see you have two speeding tickets.
Applicant: Yes.
I: Can you tell me what happened?
A: They were both on country roads.
I: How fast were you going?
A: Just 65.
I: 65 mph in what type of speed zone?

The more open you are initially with the interviewer about a specific problem area, the less concern the interviewer may have about the situation.

Interviewer: I see you have two speeding tickets.
Applicant: Yes, sir. The first ticket was going 65 in a 55, the second for going 30 in a 25. Prior to those two tickets I had not had a ticket in 10 years of driving.

WHAT IF THERE REALLY ARE NO SPECIFIC PROBLEM AREAS IN MY BACKGROUND?

I have had a few clients that truly did not have any problem areas. These people still did not escape being "grilled." If there is not a glaring area of weakness, the interviewer will make one up! (One client was chastised for making a D in freshman algebra—even though his final GPA was a 3.0). This is done because the interviewer must see how you react when confronted. It is a necessary part of the interview. The interviewer must feel comfortable that you will handle yourself as a professional even when pushed into a corner. They will be looking to see if you become defensive or if you discuss the situation with the interviewer in a positive, mature, calm manner.

The interviewer must see how you react when confronted.

Once again, it is important to remember they are not doing this because they like or dislike you. It is simply a part of the process.

It is impossible here to discuss every potential problem area. However, by following these rules and suggestions almost every mistake can be made to appear less hazardous. Most important, by following these suggestions you will be assured of being given every consideration.

NOTE:

To learn more about problem areas read *Reporting Clear?* by Cheryl Cage. To confidentially discuss a problem area with Cheryl Cage call 1-888-899-CAGE to set an appointment.

Notes

Chapter 7

PHYSICAL PRESENTATION

Now is the time to take an honest look at the kind of overall impression you make. Ask yourself and a (trusted) friend these questions:

- Do I give the appearance of good health?

- Is my hair cut stylishly and neatly?

- Are my hands and fingernails neat and clean?

- Does my interview suit fit me perfectly?

- Are my shoes businesslike, comfortable, and polished?

- Are my glasses stylish?

Interview Attire

You not only want to sound the part of a professional airline pilot, you want to look the part. Make it easy for the interviewer to picture you in the airline's uniform.

MEN

☐ To any pilot interview you must wear a business suit. It is best to select a dark color (navy, black). Wear a white shirt, black shoes and socks, and a fashionable but conservative tie. Make certain your shoes are shined and don't squeak!

☐ Try on your interview suit a few weeks prior to the interview. Don't make the mistake of thinking, "Oh, they'll never notice the pants are too short, or the jacket sleeves are frayed." The interviewer WILL notice.

☐ Have your hair cut no more than 3 days prior to the interview.

☐ Make sure your nails are clean and groomed. (If you bite your nails—stop now!)

- [ ] Keep accessories to a minimum. A wedding ring, watch, tie clip (make sure it is small—no big gold jets!) are acceptable. No bulky bracelets or chains.

- [ ] Do not wear cologne or after shave. You never know who may have allergies.

- [ ] Carry a briefcase or a business folder (no bulky flight bags!).

WOMEN

- [ ] Although the airline uniform for a female pilot is pants, it is still expected business attire to come to the interview in a suit with a skirt.

  Although you want the length of your skirt to be fashionable, it is a good rule of thumb not to have the hem more than two inches above the knee.

  You may, however, wear a coordinated pants suit (pants and jacket) to the simulator ride.

- [ ] Keep the color of your suit conservative (blue, black, gray, tan, etc.)

- [ ] Wear nude or black colored hose. (Wear black only if your skirt and shoes are black, otherwise stick to nude.)

- [ ] Keep make up and jewelry to a minimum.

- [ ] Small stud earrings (gold, pearl, diamond) are acceptable, as are a wedding ring and watch. You may find a strand of pearls or a slender gold chain compliments your suit, but stay away from big costume jewelry, heavy pins, and bracelets.

- [ ] Make up should be hardly noticeable. No heavy eye shadows.

☐ Do not wear perfume or cologne (you never know who has allergies).

☐ If you wear heels make certain that you can walk comfortably on carpet, and that the heel of the shoes does not make too much noise on a hard surface floor. It has been my experience if you get heels higher than 1 1/2 inches you may tend to wobble.

☐ If you carry a briefcase do not carry a purse. Carrying more than one case can make you appear awkward.

☐ Keep your nails short and well-groomed. Use no polish or clear polish. A French manicure is acceptable if your nails are short.

☐ Your hairstyle should fit your face. A good rule of thumb is to keep your hair away from your face. If it is long, pull it back in a French braid or bun. Stay away from "big" hair and too much styling gel.

☐ Keep an extra pair of pantyhose with you!

MISCELLANEOUS

☐ Do not accept any coffee or tea during the interview. You do not need the added stress of handling a hot drink.

☐ It is fine to accept, and drink when needed, a glass of water.

MEN and WOMEN

Handshake

A limp handshake accompanied by poor eye contact does not make a good first impression. It is better to have a handshake that is a little too firm rather than too relaxed.

Here are some tips for a professional handshake. These tips are applicable whether you are meeting a man or a woman.

- Don't be afraid to extend your hand first.
- Make eye contact the whole time you are being introduced.
- Smile!
- Take the person's whole hand in yours. Make sure your thumb is aligned with the other person's wrist.
- Make sure you can feel the other person's whole hand. If you are touching all the pressure points, the handshake should feel firm without crushing bones.
- Hold the handshake for as long as it takes to say, "It's a pleasure to meet you," then release.

Sweaty hands

While you are waiting, keep your hands unclenched and let the air circulate around them.

Right before you meet someone, press your palm against your pants leg or skirt. The material will absorb a little bit of the excess moisture. Your hand may still be moist, but not dripping wet.

Smoking

Do not smoke, or be around smoke, in your interview clothing. Do not smoke the day of the interview.

I met with a client who smelled strongly of cigarette smoke. Being a non-smoker, by the end of our session together I had quite a headache. I suggested to him that he needed to have his suit dry-cleaned and mentioned he should not smoke around his interview clothing and paperwork. He looked surprised and said, "I don't smoke." It turned out his wife smoked. Even though they thought they had been careful by keeping his clothing and paperwork in the guest room, the cigarette smell was still very strong.

The Mock Interview

- ## The Key to a Polished Presentation

A videotaped mock interview is one of the most important and beneficial preparation processes.

Watching yourself on videotape allows you to take a "third party" look at yourself. You will clearly notice that your tone of voice became a bit sarcastic when you answered that question about your first flying job. You will see that you spent the majority of the time looking at the floor or the ceiling, and you will notice that as time went by you appeared to sink into your chair!

Because my clients could see in five minutes what it had been taking me two hours to try to explain, videotaping the mock interviews immediately knocked two hours off my interview sessions with pilots. So, when you are ready to do a mock interview I want you to beg, borrow, or steal (no, don't do that, who needs another problem area?) a video camera!

CONDUCTING A MOCK INTERVIEW

- ### The Interviewer

Pick an "interviewer" who is familiar with aviation and who is someone you trust to give you honest feedback. In order for the individual to fully understand the learning process you are going through have them read through the workbook, paying special attention to problem areas.

- ### Dress

Set the stage to mirror the interview atmosphere. Wearing jeans and a t-shirt will set too casual a tone. It is best to wear your interview suit, but at the very least wear a coat and tie (for men) or a skirt and blouse (for women).

- **Stage**

  Once again, set the stage correctly. You should sit in a straight back chair. Have the interviewer sit in a more comfortable chair, or behind a desk. The interviewer should sit next to the camera. You should be the only person on camera.

- **Camera view**

  Be careful of the lighting of the room. Make sure you have the light straight ahead of you. Do not have a lamp in back of you or to the side (your face would be in shadow).

  The camera should give a clear view of you from the knees up. (By including your knees you will be able to tell if you are crossing/uncrossing your legs, fidgeting in your chair. You will be able to critique your whole body stance.)

- **Questions**

  Enclosed in this workbook are examples of interview questions. To best simulate an interview the interviewer should select the questions at random. Also, provide your interviewer with a copy of your airline application.

  It will be the interviewer's responsibility to ask follow up questions, or to challenge you on problem areas.

- **Review**

  After the mock interview, ask your interviewer for his initial reactions. Discuss how you felt and where you sensed you did well or not so well. After your discussion, review the tape together. Stop the tape whenever you see a problem.

- Additional mock interviews

  Although this is a necessary and helpful exercise it is important not to overdo it. It is my policy never to do more than two mock interviews.

  One mock interview should be done at the beginning of your preparation—after working through the workbook once. The second interview should be done a week later, after you have had time to dissect your initial responses and have worked through the rough areas.

Notes

Chapter 8

PAPERWORK PRESENTATION

Imagine for a moment that your first choice airline has *finally* invited you for an interview.

The big day arrives. You are ushered into the interview room, offered a chair and asked for your paperwork.

You give the interviewer your documentation. After a few moments of review, the interviewer looks up, leans back in his chair, and says, "Why haven't you listed all the phone numbers of your past employers?" or "Do you know you forgot to sign the back of the application?"

Sit back and imagine how off-balance you would feel.

A pilot interviewer once told me of a board of review he attended when he was in training to conduct interviews. The board was trying to decide between two individuals, Bob and Joe. Same experience, education, and training. Copies of both applicants' paperwork had been passed around. The job was finally given to Joe because his paperwork was more professionally presented than Bob's. Bob had spelled several words wrong and had neglected to provide his complete employment history.

Never forget—your paperwork will be reviewed by people who will never meet you. You will have no chance to explain mistakes or deletions to these individuals. You will be judged strictly on your paperwork!

Forgetting to sign the application, having the dates wrong on your job history, listing flight time incorrectly, misspelling words, poor grammar, not having all the requested documents—these are the type of errors that can cost a job offer.

Fortunately, careful planning and extensive review can help decrease these mistakes.

Take another second, and imagine yourself back in that interview room. Except this time after several moments of reviewing your paperwork the interviewer looks up, smiles and says, "Well, everything seems to be in order. So, let's move on."

Feels great, doesn't it?

Your paperwork is "you" on paper. If done correctly, it will be a tremendous asset during the interview process. If done poorly, it could cost you a job offer.

Resume

☐ Your resume should be one page only.

☐ Use white or light ivory colored paper, 25 lb., 100% cotton. Use the same paper for your resume and cover letters.

☐ Have your resume professionally designed and printed.

☐ Do not put the word "resume" on your resume.

☐ Do not leave employment gaps of more than 2 months.

☐ Do not include references on your resume. You may put references on a separate page.

- Headings that must be included (see the resume example on page 72):

    1. *Flight Time*

        You may wish to break down your time the same way the airline asks it to be listed on the company application.

    2. *Ratings and Certifications*

    3. *Experience*

        You may choose any title or word to describe this section (experience, work experience, work history, etc.). Use the term "Aviation Experience" if you are listing aviation jobs only.

List primarily your adult work history. If you worked during high school/college these jobs would be listed under EDUCATION and mentioned in the context of paying for school, etc.

EXAMPLE: B.S. in Aviation Management, Metropolitan State College, Denver, Colorado. To pay for college/flight training worked all four years as a fueler/scheduler for Wings Above FBO.

4. Education

If you have a college degree, you need not list your high school information.

- Additional headings that may be included:

1. Specialized Training

EXAMPLE: Aerobatic Training Course (2 weeks), ABC Aviation, Centennial Airport, Englewood, Colorado.

2. Community Involvement/Volunteer Experience

EXAMPLE: Boy Scout Leader for Troop 56 (1992–94), Miami, Florida.

3. Hobbies/Interests

EXAMPLE: Restore antique cars for resale. Sell one car every two years.

4. Honors/Awards

EXAMPLE: Instructor of the Month (2/93, 4/93), ABC Aviation.

Some airlines electronically scan resumes. If this is the case make sure the resume you send meets the airline's scanning requirements.

Feel free to use as many of these headings as is applicable to your situation. However, keep your resume one page.

Items such as height, weight, age, family situation, non-smoker are not applicable. A good rule of thumb for these types of personal items is that if the airline does not ask the question on the application, do not put it on your resume.

The statement of availability or references is not needed. I usually only use this one line statement to balance out the look of the resume (see example).

The Application

The airline application will be the primary information source for the interviewer. For this reason it is important to use all available space to point out your background and experience.

- Unless it specifically states to print, always type your application or hire a professional to do it for you. (Never have someone else print the application for you!)

- Leave no questions unanswered or any spaces blank. If a question is not applicable to your situation (military service, foreign languages spoken) write "n/a" or "none."

- Use exact numbers when listing flight time.

- Send only the information that is requested. Do not bulk up your application packet with letters of reference and copies of commendations. You may present that information during your interview.

- Do not expect the interviewer to do the research for you. For example, it is not acceptable to list "not known" under a request for the address of a former employer.

Send only the information that is requested.

If a past employer's current address is unknown supply the interviewer with a secondary contact. This secondary contact could be the address of your former supervisor, or the address of the corporation that bought out your employer, or (at the very least) the address of a former co-worker who can verify your employment. If you are using a secondary contact, make your W-2's, training records, etc., available at the interview.

- Most airline applications ask "interview" type questions on their applications. Questions such as these are great openings to point out special traits or experiences.

Some examples:

☐   List civic, social, or professional organizations which have provided you with job related skills.

Remember that job related skills are not just aviation skills! You probably learned a great deal about teamwork from playing on the basketball team at college, from working on your Homeowners Association, or from coaching your child's Little League team.

☐   What honors or awards have you received?

Make sure you list that four-year language scholarship, point out the fact that you were selected to study overseas. If you have been selected employee/volunteer/instructor of the month/year put it on your application!

☐   What else would you like us to know about you?

You are striving to allow the interviewer to know the "real" you, the whole individual. You don't just fly airplanes! Use these "interview" questions to list those non-aviation related interests, hobbies, memberships, and awards!

JOHN J. WRIGHT
Social Security: 010-10-1010

Permanent Address
555 Aviation Way, #B-727
Dallas, Texas 45456

Contact Numbers
Home: (555) 988-5511
Alternate: (555) 767-7676

OBJECTIVE

Flight Officer with ABC Airways

FLIGHT TIMES

Total Time:	xxxx
Pilot in Command:	xxxx
Multi-Engine:	xxxx
Instrument:	xxxx

RATINGS

Airline Transport Pilot
Type Rating: B-737
Commercial Privileges: ASEL, AMEL
Certified Flight Instructor: Multi-Engine, Instrument
FAA First Class Medical Certificate: No restrictions

EXPERIENCE

08/99 to Present

Dallas Express Airlines
1212 Midway Ct.
Dallas, TX 45456

Captain/First Officer: BAe-146. Part 121 passenger operations throughout midwest.

07/96 to 07/99

Corporate Charter, Inc.
23 Wildwood Ave.
San Diego, CA 45322

First Officer: SAAB-340. Passenger service within California and Arizona.

06/95 to 07/96

ABC Flight School
41 Willow St.
Los Angeles, CA 45332

Flight Instructor: Commercial, Instrument.

EDUCATION

University of Colorado
Boulder, Colorado
Dean's List: 4 years.

Bachelor of Science in Aviation Technology

PROFESSIONAL TRAINING

January 2000

South Training Academy

Type Rating: Boeing 737

AVAILABILITY

Immediate, however, two weeks notice preferred.

Cover Letters

Your cover letters should be addressed to a specific person if possible (director of personnel, chief pilot, whoever is in charge of hiring).

Your cover letter should consist of one page which includes three short paragraphs.

Paragraph 1: Who you are and why you are writing (1-3 sentences).

After fifteen years of service I recently separated from the Air Force. I have enclosed my application and would appreciate being considered for a pilot position with American Airlines.

Paragraph 2: Specific experience that is valuable to the particular airline (4-7 sentences).

I received my bachelors degree in aeronautical engineering from the University of Colorado. After graduation I entered the Air Force. For the last three years of my tour I have been flying as Commander on the C–140 and accumulated over 2000 hours of PIC time. This position has allowed me to fly throughout the U.S., Canada, South America, and Europe.

Paragraph 3: Closing statement (2-4 sentences).

I believe my experience as a pilot and my record as an employee would make me an asset to American Airlines. Thank you for considering my application. I hope to hear from you soon.

Close your letter using a standard salutation (sincerely, respectfully).

NOTE: A word about corporate resumes and cover letters

If you are pursuing a corporate pilot position, the resume and cover letter take on a bit more importance than a standard airline resume and cover letter. This is because the airlines primarily follow the company application form when reviewing documents and interviewing an applicant. Corporate flight departments may not even have a company application. Thus, they will use the resume and the cover letter when reviewing documents and interviewing an applicant. For this reason you should expand your resume to include several of the miscellaneous headings if possible.

Your cover letter will need to be more in-depth than a standard airline cover letter. The second paragraph is where you will expand the text.

IMPORTANT! IMPORTANT! IMPORTANT!

—Always, always, always keep copies of ALL the paperwork you send to an airline. Keep copies of resumes, applications, references, cover letters!

—Always include an "application received" self-addressed, stamped postcard. This will alleviate worrying whether the airline received your application packet.

Chapter 9

INFORMATION GATHERING

Putting together all the information and documentation required by an airline is a time intensive task which requires complete accuracy. This task can be made much easier if you gather all the required information prior to beginning the actual process of preparing your resume and completing your applications.

Gathering this information early will also allow you to solve any problems or mistakes you discover along the way. Problems can range from an error on your driving record to the discovery that your college registrar's office has never heard of you! I have had too many clients receive their FAA records three days before the interview only to discover an error. VERY STRESSFUL!

DOCUMENTATION

☐ Request your airman's record from the Federal Aviation Administration in Oklahoma City, OK. Call 1-405-954-4173, FAX 405-954-4655.

☐ Write away for your driving record from the state department of motor vehicles.

☐ Gather all the originals of your licenses and make clear copies.

☐ Obtain your educational records. Make sure you have a sealed copy to present to the interviewer.

☐ Make sure your passport is up-to-date.

FLIGHT TIME	☐ Make sure your log books are up-to-date.
	☐ Break down your flight time (instructor, multi, captain, first-officer, simulator, dual, etc.).
	☐ List all certifications and ratings.
	☐ Compile all training records.

IMPORTANT! List your flight time the way the airline requests it—not the way the FAA, or the military, or your friends say you can list it. You can lose a job offer if it appears you have padded your flight time in any way.

Also, be careful of personal comments listed in your logbook. Writing a comment such as, "the captain I flew with today was a jerk" does not say good things about your professionalism.

WORK HISTORY	☐ List all your work history in reverse chronological order, beginning with most recent and ending with freshman year in high school. Include the dates of your employment, the company name, job title and duties, and salary.
	☐ List reasons for leaving each job (return to school, advancement, company furlough, etc.)
	☐ List names, addresses and phone numbers of each employer.
	☐ If you have more than 30 days between jobs (when you were not in school), list the reasons why.
	☐ Collect letters of reference from as many employers as possible.
	☐ List any awards or achievements received through your employment (i.e.,employee of the month).
	☐ Gather letters of recommendation from personal references.
EDUCATION	☐ List all your formal education in reverse chronological order. Include any degrees received and/or the area of study as well as the name of the school with the city and state.

CHECKLIST FOR SUCCESS

☐ List any awards or achievements in school (e.g., outstanding GPA of 3.3 or above, scholarships, academic contests won, school offices held, sports played, etc.).

☐ If you paid for part or all of your education list how this was accomplished (e.g., full/part time work during school).

SPECIALIZED TRAINING

☐ List any specialized aviation training you have completed on your own (e.g., mountain flying, aerobatics programs).

COMMUNITY INVOLVEMENT

☐ List any past or present volunteer experience. Include your volunteer title, the name of the organization, and your basic duties.

☐ List any awards or honors received through your volunteer work.

INTERESTS OR HONORS

☐ List any hobbies or interests.

Be specific if you have unusually in-depth interests or interests which are applicable to flying. This section is for honors or awards which do not fit under the headings of EDUCATION or WORK HISTORY.

HINT: If you are wondering if you should list a certain hobby or interest ask yourself this question: If I am asked to discuss this interest/hobby can I have an in-depth discussion about this subject?

IMPORTANT! Always keep a copy of each document, letter of reference, resume, and application for your records!!!

Resume Worksheet

Use this worksheet to organize the information you have collected.

As you fill out the worksheet, you will begin to see what information is most important to include.

Flight time

Total time _____

Breakdown of Time: Personal preference as to how you will break down your total time, i.e., PIC, Multi-engine, Instructor, etc. A good rule of thumb is to use the same breakdown as the airline's application form.

PIC Time: _____

Multi Engine Time: _____

Other: _____

Ratings & Certifications _____

_____

_____

Employment History

Job Title _____

Dates Employed/Salary _____

Name of Company _____

Address of Company _____

Job Description _____

Job Related Honors _____

Job Title _____

Dates Employed/Salary _____

Name of Company _____

Address of Company _____

Job Description _____

Job Related Honors _____

Job Title _____

Dates Employed/Salary _____

Name of Company _____

Address of Company _____

Job Description _____

Job Related Honors _____

Education

Degree   _____

College or University   _____

Academic Honors/Special
Accomplishments   _____

College Work History
(if applicable)   _____

Degree   _____

College or University   _____

Academic Honors
Special Accomplishments   _____

College Work History
(if applicable)   _____

Specialized Training

Type of Training   _____

School Attended   _____

Type of Training   _____

School Attended   _____

Volunteer Experience

Job Title _____

Title of Organization _____

Duties _____

Job Title _____

Title of Organization _____

Duties _____

Honors & Interests

Use an extra heading only if your honors or interests do not fit under other categories. For example, academic scholarships would go under Education, volunteer awards could go under Volunteer Experience.

Honor Title _____

Organization _____

Interests _____

Hobbies _____

Notes

Chapter 10

FROM THE PROFESSIONALS

The Pilots

The following is a listing of comments and advice from major carrier airline pilots who have held positions as flight officer interviewers for their airlines.

TECHNICAL

Basic areas covered in the technical portion of the interview will usually include:

- weather

- regulations

- computations

- airplanes flown

- logbooks

The pilot interviewer will review your application, resume, and logbooks to gauge your experience level.

The specific questions asked within these areas will depend on the experience level of the applicant.

- Regardless of experience level the applicant should be a "pro" on the airplane they are currently flying, be it a Cessna–172 or a B–747, or any airplane that they have extensive experience flying.

- Many people can give details such as wing span, gross weight, fuel capacity, etc., of the airplanes they have flown. But what will really impress a pilot interviewer is for an applicant to be able to discuss in detail the systems and the idiosyncrasies of an aircraft.

- The pilot interviewer will review your application, resume, and logbooks to gauge your experience level. The pilot interviewer has the freedom to ask a variety of technical questions. If you have flown a rare type of aircraft do not be lulled into complacency and believe that questions will not be asked on that aircraft. The pilot interviewer has a wealth of information at his fingertips—a library of manuals, access to pilot instructors at the airline training department, etc. It only takes him a moment to make a call before the interview and obtain information about a certain aircraft in order to be able to ask specific, detailed questions to test your knowledge.

- One of the most common areas of weakness is in reading approach and route charts. Make sure you are comfortable with chart symbols, numbers, etc.

GENERAL

- Neatness and accuracy count! An application/resume that is not neatly filled out (directions not followed, poorly typed or hastily hand-written, typographical and grammatical errors), says to the interviewer, "This applicant will be sloppy in the cockpit," or, "This applicant obviously does not care very much about this job."

- Logbooks must be up-to-date and neat. Sloppy, disorganized logbooks will be the cause of a great deal of questioning and concern on the part of the interviewer.

Do not be afraid to admit that you were wrong.

- If you have a violation or an accident/incident on your record do not be afraid to admit that you were wrong. Discuss your error and let the interviewer know how it happened and what you learned from this mistake. Give an example of how you have incorporated this lesson into your flying since the event.

- Pilot interviewers will ask situational questions. It is frustrating to have to pull information out of an applicant. It is also frustrating, as well as not believable, when an applicant insists he has never had a conflict with a captain/supervisor, has never disagreed with a captain/supervisor, or has never had a disagreement with a co-worker. Without a frank discussion of past experiences and lessons learned, the interviewer will have no choice but to make a negative decision because the applicant provided "no information/insufficient information."

- Practice your interviewing skills.

- Don't neglect to research the airlines history and future plans.

SIMULATOR

- Invest money in practice sessions in a simulator.
- Practice in a simulator as similar as possible to the one the airline uses to test applicants. This way the procedure/profile/feel of the simulator will be fresh in your mind. If possible, become familiar with the profile you will be asked to fly.

Tighten up your standards.

If there is no simulator similar to the one the airline will be using to test you, there are other ways to prepare (although you should do these things in addition to simulator time):

- Work on your instrument flying skills.
- Shoot approaches.
- Tighten up your standards. Some pilots feel satisfied with +/- 50 feet on altitudes. That could cause problems on a simulator test ride.

FLIGHT TIME

- Do not send in your application to an airline until you are positive you have listed your flight time correctly.
- Do not guess on your flight time. Do not round numbers up.
- Do not include anticipated flight time.
- Do not become confused with what the FAA allows to be logged versus how the airline wants your time to be presented.

The Personnel Professionals

The following is a listing of general advice and answers to some specific questions by airline hiring professionals from several major carriers (American, Northwest, United, and US Airways).

GENERAL

During the personnel part of the interview we try to assess: Does this applicant have an enthusiastic attitude? Is this applicant a team player? Will this applicant speak up in critical situations?

(Our airline) is hiring future captains and role models. We want excellent technical pilots who communicate well—speaking or listening, who have demonstrated effective problem-solving and decision-making abilities, who show the command ability to become a captain, and who possess good stress management skills.

QUESTION: *What are you trying to learn when reviewing an applicant's background in the areas of . . .*

. . . EDUCATION

We look at the level of education—most successful candidates have completed a four-year degree. We check for frequent changes in universities or majors. Why did the applicant keep switching? If he began college but did not complete a degree, what was the reason for leaving school? We examine college grades because weak academics could indicate future training problems.

Although it is not required, a technical degree might be helpful because it is easier for an individual to adapt to pilot training if he has already mastered some technical information.

. . . WORK HISTORY

We look for career progression. We want to know whether the candidate's job changes were made so that he could increase his qualifications and gain a variety of flight experience. Also, we check for gaps in employment and have the candidate explain his activities during those time periods. The candidate's current job should be commensurate with other individuals who have similar flight time and qualifications. (Obviously, consideration is given to the current economic situation in the airline industry.)

. . . EXTRA CURRICULAR ACTIVITIES

These activities give an indication of a well-rounded person; they show leadership and self-directed behavior. Extra curricular activities are probably more important for the inexperienced pilot who does not have a proven work history and has few flight hours. For recent graduates of college aviation programs, participation in Alpha Eta Rho or being on the school's flight team helps create a positive impression.

. . . FLIGHT TRAINING

We review the applicant's civilian and military flight training. If his training is civilian, we want to know what type of training program he went through. Formal, structured courses are preferable. We will check for a normal progression through the various ratings and probe any failed checkrides or gaps in his training.

QUESTION: *What situations in the above areas cause you the most concern?*

ANSWER: Unsafe practices and dishonesty.

QUESTION: *What if an applicant has:*
a) not upgraded at the earliest possible opportunity?

ANSWER:
a) Not upgrading at the earliest possible time can be questioned as lack of commitment to career or viewed as possible training problems. Overall, it does depend on the circumstances.

b) failed a checkride?

b) Failing a checkride can be considered a negative, but it depends on when in his flying career it happened, what part of the checkride he failed, and if he re-took it and passed.

c) failed an upgrade or yearly proficiency?

c) These situations are considered very serious.

QUESTION: *When reviewing a beginning pilot's background, is the length of time in which ratings are accumulated important?*

ANSWER: Yes. In a way, it shows commitment, drive and motivation when an individual receives his ratings in a continuous and appropriate time period.

QUESTION: *Do test scores on flight tests carry a great deal of importance?*

ANSWER: Not much, due to the variety of cram courses available. A person can cram and forget the information the next week. However, low scores are not impressive, and there is really no excuse for a low score.

QUESTION: *What advice would you give a displaced airline pilot or a former military pilot applicant?*

ANSWER: Maintain your flight currency. If you are coming from the military, obtain civilian ratings if possible. You should stay focused on continuing your flying career. In other words, don't quit flying and choose computer programming as an alternate career if flying doesn't happen to work out right away. Stay focused on obtaining a flying position. Don't set your goals to only work for a major carrier—take any flying job that is available. Don't feel it's beneath you to take a commuter job. Bottom-line: display a commitment to continue your flying career, no matter what it takes.

QUESTION: *What is the most common mistake displaced airline pilots or former military pilots make during an interview?*

ANSWER: Assuming their flight experience speaks for them. They show a lack of preparation for the interview and are not taking the interview process seriously enough. They don't present the requested documentation.

QUESTION: *Would you share some 'interesting' or 'funny' interview experiences that contributed to a negative interview?*

ANSWER:

- One candidate, when asked what he enjoyed most about flying, responded, "It's the most fun I can have with my pants on."

- Another candidate, when trying to demonstrate his point during the interview, stood up, raised his arms to simulate airplane wings, and "flew" around the office while giving his explanation of the event.

- One candidate asked the interviewer how her suit looked, said that she had borrowed it from her sister, and did it look too big? She then asked the interviewer if she minded if she took her hair down, and proceeded to remove it from the 'bun' hairstyle it was in. She placed the hairpins on the interviewer's desk.

- A candidate was asked about discrepancies in his application and responded, "I never look at applications when I'm filling them out."

- An applicant brought his own can of Coke with him and drank it during the interview. He burped softly several times.

- In the middle of the interview an applicant asked the interviewer for a refill on his coffee.

- A male candidate sent a picture of himself in a bathing suit to prove "that he was in great shape".

Whatever you do, DON'T CHEW GUM.

The Medical Exam

Suggestions on how to prepare for the medical exam can only be general in nature. If you have a medical problem or question consult with your physician.

1. A week before an interview is not the time to decide to make changes in your lifestyle! Think long-term and keep current on your state of health. Exercise and eat right.

2. It is imperative that you always be completely honest on your FAA medical application and airline medical questionnaires. The discovery that you neglected (for whatever reason) to list some required information or failed to disclose requested background facts will likely result in your being denied a job offer or having a previous job offer rescinded.

3. If you have an uncommon medical situation (accident with injury, past health problems, etc.) make sure that you collect all applicable documentation. You want to be able to present this documentation to the airline medical examiner if it is requested.

Recently, the Americans With Disabilities Act (ADA) was signed into law. The most noticeable change as a result of the ADA is that now an airline will extend a job offer contingent upon the applicant passing a medical examination. This means you will not have to take a medical examination prior to having a job offer extended. This modification serves as proof the importance of keeping abreast of any changes which may affect the standards for the airline pilot pre-employment medical.

Chapter 11

COMMON APPLICANT CONCERNS

Answers to the questions I am most frequently asked by clients.

1. What happens if the interviewer asks a question and I simply do not know the answer (technical or personal)?

Remember—NO ONE has a perfect interview. It is very likely that you WILL encounter a question for which you are not able to give a sufficient answer. However, even when you don't have a complete answer you can still make a positive impression.

Never say "I don't know" to any question. If you do not know the answer, explain WHY you don't have any information to share.

For example, the interviewer is trying to discover how you handle problems with co-workers and asks the following question:

"Tell me about a fight you had with a ticket agent (or flight attendant, or mechanic)."

Your dilemma is that you have never been in a situation where you fought with someone in the position described.

Instead of replying "I can't think of anything" (which leaves the interviewer with the feeling that you perhaps CAN think of something but you're just not talking), offer to discuss a situation that closely resembles the question asked. This will still allow you to give the interviewer some insight into how you handle problems with co-workers.

If you are faced with this situation, let the interviewer know that you realize that your answer is not exactly what was requested. You do not want to appear as though you are trying to rewrite the questions being asked. For example:

"I don't recall ever being in a situation where I actually fought with a ticket agent. However, if you would like, I can talk about a difference of opinion I had with a fellow pilot that I found stressful."

If the question you are struggling with is a technical question, the same statement holds true. Try NEVER to say "I don't know." If you are questioned on an FAR and are unable to remember the specifics of the rule, but you do remember in what section of the FAR manual you could find the rule—share that information with the interviewer.

If you absolutely, positively cannot think of ANYTHING to say be straightforward and professional. No hemming and hawing. Look the interviewer in the eye and say "Sir, I am sorry but I am unable to come up with an answer for that question."

2. What if I need to re-schedule my interview?

- If the airline offers you a choice of dates:

When you choose your interview day, select a date that allows you enough time to fully prepare. After the commitment is made, the only acceptable reason to reschedule is your own illness or a death or serious illness in your family. If you must reschedule, have the dates of your availability in front of you when you call the airline. Reschedule as soon as possible. Be prepared for the possibility that the airline will have no dates available (it may be that you are at the end of their hiring phase). You will have to decide, right then ON THE PHONE, whether you will keep your original appointment or cancel and take your chances for a later date.

- If the airline simply assigns you a day and time to interview:

You should first try to work your other commitments around the interview. If that absolutely does not work, call the airline and tell them of your schedule conflict (you have to fly for your current airline, etc.) Have your availability dates in front of you.

It has been my experience that all airlines are very helpful the first time you need to reschedule (for the right reason). However, they will start to question your motivation should you need to reschedule more than once.

3. How do I present additional documentation that I feel is important when the airline has not requested it?

There are several ways to handle this without appearing to be inundating the interviewer with additional paperwork.

- Wait for the right question during the interview.

Let's suppose you have two letters of recommendation you feel are outstanding, but the airline does not ask for letters of recommendation. During your interview the interviewer asks: "How would your former employers describe you?" Your response might go something like: "They would describe me as extremely dependable and easy to work with. In fact, I have two letters from past employers I would be happy to leave with you."

If the interviewer says, "Yes, I would like to see them." Great!

If the interviewer declines, at least he knows you were thinking about the interview enough to organize additional documentation!

OR

- You can wait until the end of the interview.

When the signal is given that the interview is coming to an end (Thank you for your time, Do you have any questions, etc.) speak up, "Mr. Smith, I have some additional paperwork concerning my background I would like to leave with you, if I may."

Once again, whatever the answer you will come across as an organized, well prepared individual!

4. Is it acceptable to use first names?

It is acceptable to use first names if you are specifically invited to do so. IF NOT, always use Mr. or Ms!

5. What if I do not have all the requested documentation by the day of my interview?

In your paperwork packet that you will hand to the interviewer (or personnel clerk) on the day of your interview include an "Addendum" sheet which lists all missing documentation. You want to include this sheet so that ANYONE reviewing your paperwork will understand that you did not just forget to include a particular document.

For example, if your are missing your driver's license record and a certified copy of your college transcripts the addendum sheet would appear as such:

Addendum to Paperwork for John Doe
S. S. # 111-11-1111
123 First St., Anytown, CO 00000
000/555-5555

College Transcripts (Certified Copy): The documents from the University of Texas have been requested but not yet received. I have enclosed a student copy.

Driver's License Record: My Texas driving record has been requested but not yet received.

If you have old documents, such as a student's copy of your college transcripts or a year-old driver's license record, offer them. It will at least give the interviewer some of the information needed to conduct your interview.

6. Should I tell the interviewer (at my first choice airline) that I have another job offer and I need to know the outcome of my interview as soon as possible?

NO! Many clients have assumed that this type of statement in an interview shows that they are in high demand. On the contrary, you may well be viewed as pushy and a bit arrogant.

However, if you have not heard from your first choice airline, and you receive a job offer from another carrier, you may indeed call the employment office. The phone will most likely be answered by the receptionist or personnel clerk. Tell this individual your situation and ask them if it would be at all possible to discover the outcome of your interview.

The few times a client has had to do this, the airlines were exceptionally helpful. However, be prepared for them to say they are unable to give you that information (perhaps the decision has not yet been made). You will then have to make the decision with the information that is available to you.

7. What if I leave the interview and on my way home remember something I wanted to tell the interviewer? Can I call or write them?

Comments and impressions concerning the applicant are usually written immediately after the applicant departs the interview. Writing or calling with additional information will probably not make any difference in the opinion of the interviewer. However, if you spend the time and thoroughly prepare for the interview this should not happen!

8. Right before I walk in to the interview I notice an error on my resume. Should I bring this to the interviewer's attention?

NO, if it is an error in spelling or grammar.

YES, if the error makes a difference in flight time, dates of employment, level of education, number of traffic tickets.

9. I quit keeping regular logbooks when I received my ATP. What do I do now?

If you are coming straight from a commuter/corporate/flight instructor background it will weigh heavily against you if your logbooks are not current. If this is your situation be prepared for extensive questioning on this situation. Try to reconstruct your flight time using flight pay records, company records, and training records.

10. Is it acceptable to call an airline pilot employment office to ask about the status of my application or the results of my interview?

Unsolicited phone calls make additional work for already overloaded employment offices. Even if you were able to actually speak with someone it is very rare that you will get any information over the phone.

11. I always worry that my application will get lost in the mail.

Alleviate this worry by enclosing a self-addressed stamped postcard. On the message side of the postcard write or type:

> Delta Air Lines
> Pilot Application Received _____(date)
> Please drop this card in the mail. Thank you!

12. One of my past employers has gone bankrupt. I have no address or phone number. What should I do?

This is a common situation (especially if you have worked in aviation for any length of time). However, the interviewer will still need verification of employment.

It is imperative that you do the research for them. If unable to find a current address or phone number look to other sources for verification:

- W–2's

- Pay stubs

- Employee evaluations

- Training records

- Notarized letters from fellow employees or former supervisors which will state the dates of your employment (include address and phone numbers of these people).

13. What do I say when the interviewer asks me "How did you prepare for this interview?"

This can be an extremely disconcerting question if you don't understand the reasoning behind it.

Many applicants still prepare by memorizing answers, and even using stories from a friend's background. I had one client who told me a story that I had heard, verbatim, from another client the week before. When he finished I exclaimed, "This is such a coincidence! I spoke with a client last week that had the exact same thing happen to him!" He began to turn red. I then asked him, "Did that really happen to you?" Obviously, it hadn't and we had a bit of a laugh over his getting caught. But, he learned a valuable lesson—talk only about yourself and your own experiences!

It is extremely frustrating for an interviewer to be impressed with an applicant's paperwork and to have a positive first impression, only to have the applicant give memorized answers. The applicant dances around a question, philosophizes, or offers situations that the interviewer has heard six times in the last six months. The interviewer is disappointed because he thought he had a "keeper." But he has to make a negative decision on hiring simply because the applicant is unable to share specific information about himself.

"How have you prepared?" is asked to put you on notice that canned, memorized answers will not be accepted. So, go ahead and approach the question the same way you approach the whole interview, by being open and honest!

14. How do I to alleviate the horrible feeling of getting in my car after the interview and thinking, "Oh, no, I forgot to tell them about..."?

When you give a speech you always make an outline of the important points of your talk. You need this same type of outline for your interview. The interview outline is really a *Mental Checklist*.

On this *Mental Checklist* prioritize facts that you want the interviewer to know about you. Then, use the interview questions as an opportunity to point out these facts.

When the interviewer shows signs of ending the interview (Do you have any questions?, Is there anything else you would like to say?), take one last look at your *Mental Checklist*. If there are items left **briefly** say, "I appreciate your taking the time to talk with me. Before I go I would like to point out..." and then mention the remaining items. Or, "No, sir, I have no questions, however I would like you to know..."

Obviously, the items on the *Mental Checklist* will be different for everyone. Some examples of what might be applicable:

- Fluent in a foreign language.

- Paid for college through academic and sports scholarships.

- Consistently promoted ahead of schedule.

Don't ramble on at the end of the interview! One minute or less is all the time you have to mention any additional facts.

15. My logbooks are a mess! (White out, inappropriate comments, etc.) What can I do?

Messy logbooks are an indication of your attention to detail (or lack of). One remedy to a messy logbook is to rewrite your logbook. (I can hear the groans!) Rewriting your logbook says to the interviewer, "I realize the upkeep of my documentation was not professional. However, this is not the way I approach it now." CAUTION! If you rewrite your logbook you *must always* present your original logbook! Your original logbook is a legal document that must be reviewed.

16. I have lost one of my logbooks. Now what do I do?

A logbook is a legal document that lists your specific experience in order to gain flight ratings and benefits. If you have lost a logbook (even if you have 5,000 +hours!) you must strive to recreate your flight time. Here are some suggestions:

Beginning flight time can be recreated with help from your flight instructors. Try to reconstruct the dates of your lessons and the approximate number of hours you accumulated with the specific instructor. Have your instructor write these facts in a letter and have the letters notarized. Also, check your instructor's logbook to see if they listed your name in the comments section when they logged their flight time for your lessons. Copy these pages to present in an interview. Also, request your aircraft rental billing records from your flight school or flying club.

If you lost a logbook with teaching time try to track down former students. Recreate flight time by perhaps copying pages from their logbook where you signed them off.

If you lost a logbook with paid flying time gather your W-2s from that job. Ask the company where you were employed for any flight records they may have.

Finally, if your logbook was stolen, make sure you take a copy of the police report.

Recreating flight time in any of these manners most likely not be viewed as a complete legal document. But, it will show the interviewer that you realized the missing logbook was a problem.

By taking the trouble to recreate your time an interviewer may be less concerned that you simply didn't want to show them that particular logbook (for whatever reason).

17. I have two speeding tickets. They don't show up on my driving record. Do I have to inform the interviewer of them?

If there has been any paperwork processed, or if another person (friend, coworker, etc.) knows about the situation (traffic ticket, FAA investigation, suspension from work, job termination, etc.) the possibility of the problem area being discovered through a background check is extremely high. Aviation is a very small world!

Remember, your background check is not necessarily complete upon receiving a job offer. In fact, we have been contacted by several pilots who were dismissed at the very end of their new hire training due to the discovery of certain situations they had "neglected" to mention. (One pilot "neglected" to mention a non-flying job termination, another had "neglected" to mention a DUI which had occurred over eight years ago.)

If handled correctly you can recover from a problem area. However, you can NEVER recover from "neglecting" to tell the truth. As always, the best approach is to be open and honest.

Chapter 12

BEFORE / DURING / AFTER CHECKLIST

BEFORE APPLYING   Gather all documentation.

- [ ] Prepare your resume, applications, and cover letters.
- [ ] Make sure you meet the airline's medical criteria.
- [ ] Research the individual airlines.
- [ ] Prepare your interview clothing.
- [ ] Study for the technical part of the interview.
- [ ] Begin your interview preparation.

BEFORE THE INTERVIEW DATE   Prepare and organize your interview packet. Have on hand:

- [ ] Additional copies of your resume and application.
- [ ] Letters of recommendation.
- [ ] Reference list.
- [ ] Separate packet for paperwork concerning any violation/incident.
- [ ] Originals and copies of licenses.
- [ ] Pens and pencils.
- [ ] A nice briefcase or folder in which to carry your documentation.
- [ ] Pay attention to grooming details.
- [ ] Have your hair cut no more than 3 days prior to the interview.

SUGGESTIONS   If you must travel to another city for your interview, do not go at the last minute. You will find you are much more comfortable if you give yourself at least a day to settle in. Also, stay at a hotel close to the site of the interview. If you have friends in the city where your interview is taking place, resist the temptation to visit late into the evening prior to the day of your interview. Give yourself some "alone" time to focus and prepare for the next day.

Do not drink any alcoholic beverages for at least 3 days prior to the interview. You will be excited and a bit nervous, and alcohol can affect you differently during these times.

If you smoke, do not smoke around your interview clothing. Do not smoke the day of the interview! (Actually, if you smoke, QUIT! The health habits of a pilot are very important to an airline. Smoking is not looked upon as a positive.)

THE DAY OF THE INTERVIEW

Be in your "interview mode" no matter what circumstances you find yourself in (sitting in the waiting room, eating lunch between your interview and your simulator ride, etc.).

Arrive in time to fill out any additional paperwork they may have for you (15–20 minutes early).

DURING THE INTERVIEW

Pay close attention to the pronunciation of the interviewer's name and any employees you may meet.

LISTEN to the questions!

Talk pilot!

Do not attempt to 'butter up' the interviewer, or 'lighten up' the tone of the interview. Be polite, friendly, and focused on giving the most specific answers possible.

Be concise.

Be positive and enthusiastic about possible employment.

SMILE!

AFTER THE INTERVIEW

After you return to your car (or hotel room):

☐ Write down specific questions which you felt you answered well—or not so well.

☐ Describe your overall impressions. (These insights will help you through your next interview—if you need them!)

☐ Write the interviewer a BRIEF thank you note.

Do not ask for the address or how to spell their names during the interview. If you need this information ask the receptionist.

☐ Pat yourself on the back for a job well done!

Notes

Chapter 13

SAMPLE INTERVIEW QUESTIONS

Tell me a little about yourself.

How did you become interested in a career as a commercial pilot? What steps have you taken to achieve this goal?

Why do you want to work for this airline?

Tell me about your flight training.

What was the most difficult part of your flight training?

How did you finance your training?

Have you ever failed a checkride? What happened?

Tell me about the biggest work decision you have had to make.

Describe a work problem which you faced and tell me how you dealt with it.

What work policies or procedures have you found to be personally distasteful? Did you conform? Why or why not?

Tell me about a situation where you broke company policy.

Can you give me an example of a situation in which a company's policy and/or procedure was unfair to you? How did you cope with this problem?

Tell me about a time when you became involved in a problem faced by a peer or subordinate. What happened?

What was the most difficult situation you have experienced in establishing rapport with a crew member?

Describe the perfect work environment.

What was your most stressful situation?

What was the hardest decision you ever had to make?

What is the best decision you have ever made?

What is the worst decision you have ever made?

What is the biggest problem you have faced in the last 6 months?

What is the toughest decision you had to make while flying?

What is the quickest decision you have ever made?

Have you ever flown with a captain you did not like? How did you handle the situation?

Have you ever flown with a captain that you felt didn't like you? How did you handle the situation?

Tell me about a work problem that you solved.

Tell me about a conflict you had with a supervisor.

Tell me about a conflict you have had with a subordinate.

Have you ever disagreed with a decision the captain has made? What did you do?

Has a captain ever disagreed with a decision you made? What did you do?

Have you ever flown with someone you felt was unsafe? What did you do?

What leadership role are you most proud of?

Describe your style of leadership.

What mistakes have you made as a leader?

What would you do differently in handling your career?

Give me five of your strengths.

Give me five of your weaknesses.

What is your most positive/negative trait?

What do you like most about being a pilot? Least?

Have you ever been disciplined at work? What happened?

Tell me about your college career. Why were your grades so low? Why didn't you finish college?

What will you do if we do not select you?

SITUATIONAL QUESTIONS

You are flying in extremely bad weather and your captain seems unusually uncomfortable with the situation, what would you, as first officer, do?

Your captain pulls the cockpit voice recorder circuit breaker before engine start. What would you do?

You feel as though your captain has been drinking. It is one hour before flight time. How would you handle this?

What would you do if you saw a passenger being belligerent to a flight attendant?

What would you do if you saw a flight attendant being rude to a passenger? Captain being rude to a passenger?

What would you do if your captain was not following noise abatement procedures?

As captain you feel your first officer needs some improvement in a flying area. How would you approach him about this? What would you do if the f/o appears not to be taking you seriously?

What would you do if you saw a flight attendant take a bottle of wine from the flight?

The flight attendant comes to the cockpit and informs you that a passenger has too many bags and insists on keeping them onboard. What if the passenger was a frequent flyer who has flown a million miles with the airline?

Notes

Chapter 14

SURVIVING DISAPPOINTMENT

Right after graduation from college I began interviewing for a flight attendant position. I had a friend, Mary, who was also pursuing a flight attendant position with the airlines. Talk about depressing! That woman was offered a job everywhere she went!

It did not come as easily for me. I went through at least two interviews before I realized that I was making some fatal mistakes. (Once, I forgot to fill out the BACK of the application form). When those mistakes were corrected, I was offered a job by several carriers.

I learned several important lessons during my job search. One of the most important lessons I learned is that you <u>CAN</u> learn from your mistakes!

If you were dissatisfied with an answer, write down what you would have liked to have said, if you said something wonderful write it down and preserve it for posterity!

However, you can't correct mistakes unless you remember them. This is the reason I feel strongly about writing down all your impressions surrounding your interviews. Jot down specifics such as the names of the interviewers and their positions and the names of other employees you met. List the questions you were asked, and critique how you answered these questions. If you were dissatisfied with an answer, write down what you would have liked to have said, if you said something wonderful write it down and preserve it for posterity!

Although no one wants to think about a negative outcome, the reality is that sometimes it takes more than one try to land a job. If you find yourself in this situation, those written firsthand impressions will be invaluable in preparing for your next interview. It is also a reality that the number of major carriers to interview with has dwindled over the years. This is an additional reason for careful preparation for every interview.

The second lesson I learned is that, beyond learning about your competition, it does no good to constantly compare yourself to

---

other applicants. If you are invited for an interview, it means the airline feels confident you are qualified for the job! Every applicant has areas of strengths and areas of weaknesses. It may look like that 24 year old Top Gun, Ph.D. in Aeronautical Engineering doesn't have any weaknesses. Believe me, he does!

If you are invited for an interview, it means the airline feels confident you are qualified for the job.

Do not dwell on anyone else's background BUT YOUR OWN. Don't let the Marys of the world erode your confidence!

And finally, DON'T GIVE UP! I have worked with many clients who have interviewed with two and three carriers before being offered a position. But, because they were willing to take a good hard look at the reasons why they were getting interviews but not being offered a job—they finally succeeded!

INDUSTRY CIRCUMSTANCES

This workbook was written during a period of time when there was little, if any, pilot hiring taking place. However, for the three years prior to this "down" time, the majority of major carriers were in a hiring frenzy.

Regardless of industry circumstances during the time you are reading this book, remember: airline pilot hiring is a cyclical business. The airline industry has a long history of great spurts of growth followed by long periods of drought.

If there is a great deal of hiring going on, the applicant pool will become smaller every day. Your chance of being interviewed will increase every day!

If, on the other hand, the industry is at a hiring standstill, you can, and must, use this time to enhance your marketability. While waiting for hiring to begin again, increase your flight time, gain new ratings, finish your college education, gain new experiences through work or volunteer positions. Update your applications and your resume at appropriate intervals. Prepare yourself for interviews—sometimes things change quickly in the aviation industry. When the drought ends (which it always does) you will be in top form!

IN CLOSING

When the call comes to interview always recognize that you do have a great deal of control over the outcome. The final result is dependent on how you have prepared, through both your flight training and your interview preparation.

Remain motivated, positive, and focused on your career goals.

So, no matter what circumstances surround your job search it is imperative that you remain motivated, positive, and focused on your career goals.

ABOUT THE AUTHOR
Cheryl A. Cage

Cheryl Cage began Cage Consulting in 1988. Cage Consulting offers Pilot Interview Preparation Services in addition to being a small publishing house.

Since 1988 the consultants of Cage Consulting have assisted over 14,000 pilot clients in preparing for airline pilot interviews. Since 1995 Cage Consulting has published nine pilot study guides, including an interactive CD and an online training test.

Cheryl was an independent consultant to the Air Line Pilots Association (ALPA) from 1990 to 1994. During this time she presented her pilot interview preparation seminars to over 3,000 displaced ALPA pilots from PanAm, Midway, USAirways, TWA, Air Wisconsin, West Air, and Aspen Airways to name a few.

In 1994 Cheryl wrote and published her first book *Checklist for Success: A Pilot's Guide to the Successful Airline Interview. Checklist* has become the book to read when preparing for a professional pilot interview. To date, the book has sold over 25,000 copies primarily through reader referral.

In 1996 Cheryl decided to expand the publishing division of Cage Consulting and actively recruited professionals in various fields to write career books. This approach resulted *Flight Plan to the Flight Deck: Strategies for a Pilot Career* by Judy A. Tarver; *Welcome Aboard! Your Career as a Flight Attendant* by Becky S. Bock (with Cheryl Cage); and *Airline Pilot Technical Interviews* and *Mental Math for Pilots* by Ronald D. McElroy. New books are being published every year.

In 1998 Cheryl wrote her second book titled *Can You Start Monday? A 9-Step Job Search Guide - Resumé to Interview.* 2000 brought her third book *Reporting Clear?* She is currently writing her fourth book with the working title of *Problem Solved: A Guide to Better Management of Mistakes, Problems, & Conflicts.*

In May 2001 Cage Consulting introduced its first online training test for pilots. The first is Pilot E-TrainingTest—Mental Math.

Cheryl has been a columnist for the Air Force Times, Army Times, and Navy Times. She has written for *Flight Training, Air Line Pilot, Aviation for Women,* and *The Independent.* She is a regular speaker at aviation conferences including Women in Aviation, UPAS, and AEPS. American Airlines has sponsored Cheryl to present seminars on the pilot selection process and interview preparation skills.

Prior to Cage Consulting, Cheryl graduated from college with a B.A. in Psychology. She became a flight attendant for Braniff Airways. When Braniff declared bankruptcy in 1982 Cheryl made a career transition into marketing and management for a national sports company. She left this position to start Cage Consulting, Inc.

PRODUCTS AND SERVICES
by Cage Consulting, Inc.
Orders, questions, or to set an consultation appointment please call:
1-888-899-CAGE (2243)
or visit our website at: cageconsulting.com

We have two main goals at Cage Consulting. The first has been to offer an in-depth, personalized approach to interview preparation. Because of our personalized approach we often have many more requests for appointments than we can fill. Due to this fact our second goal has been to produce quality books and other study products that will allow a pilot to prepare, as much as possible, on their own.

Checklist for Success: A Pilot's Guide to the Successful Airline Interview by Cheryl A. Cage
All the advice I could provide is contained in this book. W.H. Traub (VP, UAL Flight Standards & Training, Ret.)

CHECKLIST Interview Simulator CD. Written and Narrated by Cheryl A. Cage
This is a companion piece to *Checklist* book. 1:45 minutes playing time.
Cheryl is your guide through this interactive audio/video pilot interview simulator. Watch applicants answer questions in a correct and incorrect manner and listen to the in-depth critique of each response. Also included: attire, paperwork, self-evaluation.

Airline Pilot Technical Interviews: A Study Guide by Ronald McElroy
With 23 years of flying experience Ron McElroy presents approach plates, weather, AIM, FARs, cockpit situations to analyze and mental math.

Mental Math for Pilots by Ronald McElroy
Mental math in an interview, or in the cockpit, will not be a problem after spending time with this excellent math guide. An excellent tool for any pilot!

Reporting Clear? Why every pilot should investigate their background & how to do it!
by Cheryl A. Cage
In reviewing the number of government and private agencies where your information is recorded it is imperative that each pilot applicant conduct their own background check prior to attending an interview. Do-it-yourself background check and in-depth discussion on the most common problem areas encountered by pilots and how to present them effectively in an interview.

Problem Solved:
A Guide to Better Management of Mistakes, Problems, Conflicts by Cheryl A. Cage

Pilot E-Training Test: Mental Math
Become not only proficient, but comfortable, when called upon to perform mental math!
Available ONLY online at www.cageconsulting.com

Other Cage Consulting Titles

Welcome Aboard! *Your Career as a Flight Attendant* by Beck S. Bock (with Cheryl A. Cage)

Can You Start Monday? *A 9-Step Job Search Guide* by Cheryl A. Cage (for the non-pilot)

Notes

Notes

Notes

Notes

Notes

Notes

Notes

Split Second Decision

Mistake in Cockpit

Conflict - Resolved

Not Resolved

On Ground